Stepmom Survival Guide:

Simple Secrets
to
Belonging
in a
Blended Family

By Kaitlin Marriner Brulotte

Stepmom Survival Guide:
Simple Secrets to Belonging in a Blended Family

ISBN-13: 978-0-9970968-3-5
ISBN-10: 0-997-0968-3-7

Published by: Celebrity Expert Author
http://celebrityexpertauthor.com

Canadian Address:
501- 1155 The High Street,
Coquitlam, BC, Canada
V3B.7W4
Phone: (604) 941-3041
Fax: (604) 944-7993

US Address:
1300 Boblett Street
Unit A-218
Blaine, WA 98230
Phone: (866) 492-6623
Fax: (250) 493-6603

Table of Contents

Introduction

My *natural* family had a rocky start. I distinctly remember a night when my dad came home around 1 a.m. My parents began yelling at each other downstairs, upsetting my sister and I, who were hiding at the top of the stairs. I was 5 or 6, and my sister was 4. I recall putting her back to bed, tucking her in, and reassuring her that everything would be okay in the morning. That's one of my most vivid memories: my parents fighting and me caring for my sister, who was beside herself with anxiety.

Dad was working a lot, had a budding problem with alcohol, and often didn't come home until the wee hours of the morning. After the sudden, traumatic, painful loss of their third child, Mom was in deep despair and Dad rarely came home. Our parents simply lacked the foundational relationship skills necessary to sustain this tragedy, and divorced when I was 7. One year later, our mom remarried and our dad proposed to another woman.

Our dad's fiancée lived in Oakville, so every other weekend, we drove to Oakville to visit her and her two kids. She had a boy and a girl who were around the same ages as my sister and I. There was always competition during the visit because our dad was a lot of fun; at times, my dad's fiancée and her kids got to see him more than we did. We fought for Dad's attention because we saw his new relationships as being more exciting than his relationships with each of us.

As a child of divorce, sharing your parents with strangers can be very scary—you don't want them to endure further pain and stress, and you don't want to lose them any more than you already have. I was the peacekeeper in the family, a kind of protector. When Mom started dating again, she once brought a man over for dinner. At the time, I thought I didn't like him, so I threw a bowl of spaghetti on his head.

When I was 8 years old, I welcomed my new younger brother into the family. As the oldest, I often took care of my brother and sister. Though my sister had her own challenges growing up, luckily, she experienced childhood at an emotionally age-appropriate level.

Before Mom remarried, she bought a small home for the four of us: herself, my brother, my sister, and me. As a single parent of three children, Mom did the best she could. She worked two jobs and would be exhausted when she came home. With a mom who was not always physically or emotionally available, I became independent, self-sufficient, and resilient.

I was the head of the family among the four of us: my mom, my brother, my sister, and me. That role shifted when I was 9 and my stepdad entered the picture. In the beginning, I adored him and thought he was wonderful. My stepdad was nice, fun, and made me feel secure for the first time in years.

As I became older, though, I began developing my own mind and ideas. I craved some control of my own life.

Though my stepdad's heart was always in the right place and his actions stemmed from love, back then, his rules were extremely rigid, with little room for compromise. This challenging dynamic between a stepfather and his oldest stepchild is very common in blended families where the mother has been struggling to gain control of her children after the initial divorce. We began butting heads in my early teens.

The power struggle continued throughout the rest of their marriage. We tried to get professional help for our stepfamily; however, at the time (just 20 years ago), a therapist with strong foundational knowledge in stepfamily dynamics was a rare find. I was 15 when I left home. By then, I felt like I had lost the second male love of my life. For about eight months, I lived with my grandmother.

After that, I got an apartment and bought a dog, who I named Bandit. He became my baby, my best friend, my love, and my reason for getting up in the morning. I focused on caring for him and living day by day.

Until that point, I had lived for what made others happy. Suddenly, I was free to do whatever I needed or wanted to do. Without any parents watching over me or rules to follow, I began my long search of discovering who I was and what would make me happy. As I soon realized, this was not an easy road.

Looking back, it would have been so much easier if we had received professional help for our blended family. I would not have made many of the mistakes I made as a young woman, my family would have continued our traditions and grown together, and perhaps the marriage between my mom and stepfather would not have turned into another statistic (70 percent of second marriages fail). Though my parents did the best they could with the resources they had, we now know much more about blended families, including how they can work and how they won't work.

I was always a motivated person, valuing my education and being committed to helping others. By experiencing blended family life early on, I developed the resilience, perseverance, and high levels of loyalty and commitment by which I successfully put myself through nursing school. That was only one of my noteworthy achievements, none of which someone with my backstory could have expected.

When you're part of a stepfamily, it's not all smooth sailing. You may not have chosen to have a new parent or a new stepchild, but love sometimes comes in a package deal. There is no quitting. You cannot commit to a new family and then realize it's too difficult and leave.

Just because a child doesn't want to share their mom with a new man at first, doesn't mean that that new man will disappear. If Mom decides she wants a new man in her life, that's her choice, not her child's. After all, children are meant to make the *child* decisions, and adults should be making the *adult* decisions.

The catch is that as the parent or stepparent, it is your responsibility to understand blended family dynamics relevant to your situation and gain necessary skills for the best possible outcomes for all involved. It is your responsibility to model behavior appropriately for your children to give them the tools they need in life.

No matter which way you look at it, traumatic loss exists in the stepfamily, both for the kids and for the people who got divorced in the first place. Maybe you are the stepmother and this is your first marriage, but it is your husband's second marriage. In this example, not being your husband's first wife is a big loss. If he doesn't want to have kids again, that may also be a loss for you.

Being in a healthy stepfamily does require learning positive coping mechanisms to deal with loss, grief, and pain. You cannot escape those feelings, so you must learn to manage them. After my blended family experience growing up, I vowed to never, ever be in a blended family again. I didn't want to go through that type of pain again. However, I learned how to work through those feelings, taking the steps necessary to reach the best possible outcome. *Simple Secrets to Belonging in a Blended Family* shows you the path to finding bliss for you and your blended family.

~ ~ ~ ~

I HADN'T BEEN looking for a serious relationship when I met Bryan in my mid-20's. On our second date, he told me about his very young children. We were still in the acquaintance stage, so I didn't give much thought as to what this truly meant. Who knows what the future would bring?

Dazzled by his charm, I ignored the potential painful repercussions of becoming involved in another blended family. We dated seriously for over a year before we decided to take the next step and meet his children. When faced with the choice to pursue a life with Bryan, I chose to let love blindly guide me: I became his second wife and a stepmother.

We moved in together, taking care of his daughters on a half-time basis. Adjusting to my new life was challenging. No matter how much I was included in everything, I still felt like an outsider in my own new home. From my previous experience in a stepfamily, I knew this acculturation process was tough. But when I commit to something, I see it through, and I was determined to do so then.

Through various challenges, disappointments, and unmet expectations in my new family, I began soul-searching. Was this really what I wanted? Did I really want to feel this loneliness in my own home, with my own family? Don't get me wrong; I loved my family very much. It just didn't feel… right. Something was missing.

Determined to proceed with my commitment, my soul-searching allowed me to realize that it was time I take responsibility for myself and my own happiness regardless of what transpired in our blended family. Instead of taking on everyone else's problems and trying to be *Super Stepmom*—which only resulted in disappointment, guilt, and resentment—I realized that I needed to make some internal changes and stop blaming those around me.

At that time, I hadn't realized how much my new attitude and behavior would positively affect my blended family. Through some small and larger-scale personal changes, I was able to single-handedly improve our blended family dynamics. These changes empowered me, alleviating my pain, resentment, loneliness, and overall dissatisfaction with my new blended family life.

Being part of a blended family at any capacity will never be easy; each day brings a new set of unique challenges that you never see coming. However, I believe that had I not experienced blended family life during childhood (a pivotal perspective in stepfamily dynamics that will be discussed later), I would not have had the foundational knowledge needed to help my blended family thrive.

Fortunately, there is another way, and there are more answers. With the *Stepmom Survival Guide*, stepmothers will learn from my painful experience not only how to survive, but how to thrive individually and within their blended family unit.

Small changes could make a significant difference in your personal life, marriage, and family, not to mention saving you from the financial implications of another breakup. I will teach you how to keep the new love of your life, prevent ingfromand avoid becoming part of a blended family divorce statistic.

A few changes in the way you see yourself, your family, and your role within the family can spark a ripple effect, altering the dynamics of your blended family for the better. It takes just one person: *you*!

Element #1:
Gaining an Understanding of Your Blended Family Dynamics

Early in my relationship with Bryan, when challenges arose, the easiest thing to do was find someone or something outside of myself to blame. The result was always more conflict and internal unhappiness.

By truly exploring inside myself, I recognized how my actions and unhappiness were contributing to the pain of the situation as a whole. When you also realize that all you want is to be happy and have harmony in your relationship and life, you will know that only you can make yourself happy. Do you do the things that make you happy? Now is the time to figure out what makes you happy. Is it going to the gym? Reading books? Taking a bath?

You *must* make time to do these things so that you are happy. You cannot spend all your time and energy killing yourself trying to make everyone else around you happy.

After you embrace and practice what makes you happy, what once made you unhappy will become insignificant.

Now, you are balancing daily life with what makes you happy.

Once you are able to change your mindset from blaming yourself and others to looking at the bigger picture (that you just want to be happy), it can be really easy to schedule some personal time just to do what makes you happy. You would be surprised at how doing things that make you happy will affect you, your family, and your life.

What I didn't realize early on as a stepmother was how much power I had as the woman of the household. I held a lot of power to initiate change and send out vibes that would help teach my family members how to make themselves happy.

Ultimately, you have children to raise and you want to teach them how to live a good life. I knew that if my stepchildren and husband were watching me participate in activities they knew made me happy, they would see the effect on my mood, level of tolerance and generosity, and overall degree of contentment with life. This peaceful environment will encourage them to do the same for themselves, leading to increased self-fulfillment on a personal level and as a family.Understand that you are not helpless in this situation. No matter how helpless and hopeless you feel, you have the power to make yourself happy. That happiness will always have a ripple effect on others.

By making yourself happy, you make others happy. Before, perhaps you were taking responsibility for the happiness of others before attending to your own. You must be happy in your own mind and body before you can lead others to find happiness within themselves.

To maintain my personal happiness, I choose to focus on the things that I enjoy. When at home in Ottawa, I spend one hour per day walking my dogs and working out at the gym. I get outside every day for at least an hour, regardless of whether I'm traveling. I meet my social needs at the gym and at work, and by scheduling two to three lunches each week with friends.

I spend 30 to 60 minutes daily by myself reading, writing, watching a show, or doing yoga. These things motivate me. In the summer, I cycle and kayak; in the winter, I ski. I'm pretty active, but I also love reading. I'll read two or three books a week; that's what I do before bed.

When I'm spending time with my family, it's engaged time. Before, I was always available to my blended family whenever anyone needed *anything*. While that availability was special, we took the time with each other for granted. Now I realize that by spending quality time with them instead of focusing on the number of hours I spent with them, everyone benefits more.

Normally, I'll spend one hour per day fully engaged with my family, and then two to three hours on weekends between extracurricular activities. It is much better to be really engaged for those few hours instead of always being available but not very engaged.

I am always taking courses on the side, too; that makes me happy. Right now, I'm working on a Master of Arts in Counseling Psychology.

I think it is important for everyone to have a purpose outside of the home, whether that's working at your job, volunteering, or engaging in a special project. You need to have a purpose independent of your blended family so that you have something that's just yours.

Question #1: Are You Hurting?

Attribute #1: Look at What's Going On in Your Life

In this first attribute, I want you to take five minutes to do a mental inventory of what is going on in your life. Write down your answers to the following questions. There are no right or wrong answers; this exercise is to evaluate your life.

- What's working well in your blended family?

- What's not working? What are your sources of stress?

- How much of your time is devoted to your husband and each of your children weekly? Is the division of time fair? Why or why not?

- Are you working? How many hours per week?

- What personal growth and development goals are you presently working on?

- How demanding is your job, and what are you doing to handle that stress?

- How much time per week do you spend on yourself to meet your wants and needs?

- Weekly, rate what percentage of your time is spent on the following: relationships & family, physical health, career, financial goals, spirituality, mental health, community, and lifestyle.

Each of these areas of your life contributes to the lifestyle that you lead. If you find that you are devoting too much time to a single purpose, consider how your life might be different if you changed that. Both time and the amount of energy you put into these categories will influence the steps that you take to change your life.

Attribute #2: Discover What Would Improve Your Life & Relationships

Now that you have explored how much time and energy you are spending on each area of your life, you are ready to consider what would make your relationships and lifestyle better for you. Take a moment to introspect.

How do you feel? Is there a perfect family or lifestyle scenario that you see?

When you envision your life one, five, and ten years from now, what do you see? Is it favorable? Most people have at least one or two major things in their life that they wish they could change. What would make it perfect for you?

First, know that shifting the dynamic within your blended family is possible from your position. Are you a stepmom who feels she isn't respected by her stepchildren? This dynamic can change by learning about your personal reality, followed by your roles and responsibilities in your family's structure. Recognizing these factors (your reality, roles, and responsibilities) within yourself can, in turn, affect the realities, roles, and responsibilities of your husband, children, and stepchildren.

Later on, you will have the opportunity to sit down with your family to discuss these roles, responsibilities, and other aspects contributing to your family's dynamics. You may discover various factors negatively impacting your family's success that you and they didn't know existed. Fortunately, you can learn from these and gradually replace the negative behaviors with positive ones.

Attribute #3: How Your Blended Family Supports You in This Relationship

Okay, I promise this won't *all* be questions, but this honest stage of introspection is an important step in establishing your starting point. Here, you will discover what you need to change and what you need to keep doing. Make notes for yourself while considering the following:

- Are you supportive of your blended family?

- What do you do to be supportive? What do you do to be unsupportive?

- Are there ways in which you can increase your support?

- Do you feel supported by those in your blended family?

- Do you think the support might be there, but just don't feel supported?

- Do you have outside support (parents, siblings, and friends)? How do they feel about your blended family situation? Does their opinion affect you?

- Is your partner supportive? Do you support them?

- Describe your relationship with your partner's former spouse or co-parent.

Regardless of your answers, you can find immediate support from the person who knows you best: yourself. When you are always against yourself, you cannot grow and develop as a healthy person. What can you do to build your faith and trust in yourself?

Final thoughts for you to consider include:

- To what degree do you support yourself in choosing a blended family lifestyle?
- How do you convey support to yourself?
- What you can you do to improve your autonomy and self-sufficiency?

Now is the time to learn how taking care of *you* is essential to take care of your new blended family. You have a natural ability to care for and raise children, even if they aren't yours. I know you can do this!

Attribute #4: Begin Normalizing Your Pain

Most often, the pain that you and your blended family are experiencing is normal. There is a grieving process because the family was created out of loss. It was not your stepchildren's decision to acquire a new stepmom or to go from one household to two. It may not have been your partner's decision to end the marriage to his former spouse. You may not have realized you were falling in love with a man who had children from a previous marriage—or, more likely, you didn't know how difficult blended family life would be when you married him.

Do you feel that your situation, feelings, and circumstances are normal? I can assure you that they are. Your new family is grieving the losses of full-time access to biological family members, the vision of their "perfect family," and all sense of normalcy and belonging. You are also grieving, having lost your "perfect family" scenario, the comfort of being your partner's "first," and the possibility of being part of a completely nonblended family (if you don't already have one).

Again, the pain you're experiencing is normal. Each member of your blended family has a different perspective on what is painful to them. As we know, unmanaged pain can dictate reactions and behaviors that a person would not normally exhibit. No matter the cause of pain, individuals can learn to recognize their signs and symptoms of suffering to effectively manage their pain. These new positive habits will allow you to move forward as a person and as a family—ultimately, to a happier and brighter future.

Question #2: What Are the Causes of Your Blended Family's Circumstances?

Attribute #5: Notice Who Has Been Getting the Blame

What is your attitude towards blame? Who or what do you think is the cause of this situation? Notice whether you are subconsciously blaming others or taking some of the blame upon yourself. Your attitude reflects your readiness to change and engage in self-improvement. This fifth attribute gives you an overall picture of where your family is in relation to changing.

Attribute #6: Accept the Differences between Natural Families & Blended Families

There are many differences between blended families and natural families. A natural, nuclear family started slowly and was based on foundational friendship and love, which then led to marriage. The couple had a chance to grow together before they had their children. Their family has their own identity and reality as a unit.

A blended family is different because its members have been joined through some form of traumatic loss, whether that was separation, divorce, or death. Because the blended family unit is created as a result of loss, each individual is bringing a different identity, reality, and tradition into the mix. There are:

- Mom and Dad's individual and collective realities.

- Stepmom's and Dad's individual and collective realities.

- Mom and Stepdad's individual and collective realities.

The kids are often lost somewhere in the middle, trying to establish their own individual and collective realities.

The union of a blended family can harbor many negative feelings that do not exist in natural families. While the first family often begins their union as a newly married couple—after which they plan to have children when ready—in a second marriage, the kids are already present. Kids often describe their parent's new marriage as feeling like a funeral. The bond that they shared as a nuclear family is broken or dead, and a new stepparent exists who they really wish was not there.

Many people enter their second marriage thinking, "Hooray! This is a new beginning; this second marriage is going to be a great new start for us." What they don't realize is that the slate is not clean. Much baggage accompanies each member in the blended family. Once each member begins unpacking their bags, disaster strikes. Blended families need guidance working through issues and challenges.

Second marriages have other differences from first marriages. Natural families have the advantage of genetics and biological attachment to strengthen their foundation; there is an unconditional bond simply because genetics are shared. As a stepparent, however, you might never feel that attachment or love, and your stepchild might never feel loved by you in the same way that they felt loved by their biological parents. And that's okay.

Attribute #7: Notice Whether Your Blended Family Expectations Are Realistic

What are the expectations of each family member? Does each member expect the blended family to operate the same as a nuclear family? Do they expect it to be better? Worse?

There are various scenarios where blended family members will automatically have unrealistic expectations. For example, often, stepparents will enter a blended marriage thinking, "I love my new spouse, so I'm going to love their kids." That's simply not always the case, and it takes a long time to reach that point.

Attribute #8: Create a Positive Family Dynamic

The good news is that blended family life can be very fulfilling. To create a positive blended family dynamic, each member needs to understand that each individual within the unit has different experiences from the situation they bring to the table, resulting in differing thoughts, feelings, and expectations. It is important that each person in the family learn to maintain respect by honoring each other's differences in perceptions and feelings.

Question #3: Why Is This Situation Persisting?

Attribute #9: Prevent the Damaging Effects of Conflict

Often, people say, "If the kids weren't there, the conflict wouldn't be there." In reality, however, if conflict exists between a stepparent and the kids, it is often due to the couple having an improper foundation; it may be weak or undefined and require structure.

If the foundation is weak in your blended family, the order and leadership is likely lacking; members are unaware of what is expected of them. The solution is not only to forge boundaries and create blended family structure, giving the kids a sense of security, but also to strengthen your relationship with your husband to fortify your foundation as a couple.

Attribute #10: How Destructive Communication, Criticism, & Contempt Is Harmful

Every family has their share of arguments, but it's how you choose to fight with each other that matters. There is a healthy way of fighting, and there is a detrimental way of fighting. Criticizing each other, harboring contempt and resentment, and refusing to compromise are unhealthy methods of fighting. Those tactics make it difficult to show kindness, compassion, and empathy, leaving issues unresolved.

Issues can be discussed in a productive manner by refraining from attacking each other, opening up a nonjudgmental environment, and genuinely listening without thinking about what you'll say next while others are speaking. Compromise and forgiveness of mistakes or irritating behaviors is more effective than nagging someone about every little thing; this can positively affect communication.

One of the first things to think about changing is the way that you approach problems in everyday life. If you are always on the defensive and anticipating meanness or sarcasm from others, you won't be able to hear it when others are being genuine and don't intend to make you feel bad. Before reacting, ask yourself, "Is this person really trying to hurt me?"

Opening your heart to living a life of compassion, love, and empathy will help you to let go of your defensive mindset and enjoy the goodness of each individual within your blended family unit. You can nurture this personal change by teaching yourself to notice the best traits of each person, put yourself in their shoes, and relate to them with loving kindness.

Attribute #11: Commit to Change

You've decided to read this book, which shows your budding motivation and willingness to change your situation. Full commitment and openness to change will create the environment you need. In that environment, you can embrace the suggested changes that helped me finally belong in my blended family. Your family is one of the most important things in your life. Each family member deserves your full commitment to improving your family's quality of life.

Ask yourself, "How important is it to me that this blended (already second) family stays together? What am I willing to commit to doing differently so this second marriage doesn't fail like the first one did?" More often than not, your family will say, "We really want this to survive." If you're willing to put in the work and commitment, it can be absolutely wonderful and life-changing.

Attribute #12: Take Your Emotions out of the Decision

You have various common, legitimate, positive and negative feelings right now. Contempt, resentment, and guilt are emotions often accompanied by divorce or second marriages. Along with these, you may suddenly feel second-best (next to the biological parent or stepparent), or as though you're making major sacrifices.

It is important to note that these feelings are just that: normal feelings that can be managed with proper care and guidance. Let's get your negative feelings out on the table so we can learn to accept and let go. We need to begin creating a plan instead of remaining in this cycle of negativity.

Upon exploration, there is a wide range of feelings that may arise for you. Try to keep in mind that there are varying perspectives in stepfamily life; it is beneficial to keep an open, compassionate mind when considering each perspective.

Stepmom's perspective:

"All I do is give, give, give without any recognition or appreciation. I compromise and sacrifice on every level of my new life, and still get no thanks. I'm starting to resent the fact that I'm constantly expected to 'mother' these children who have no consideration or respect for me and my life. I have other life goals and responsibilities that are suffering every time I go out of my way to make my blended family happy.

"Will there ever become a point where I can focus on myself or my own children? My husband expects me to act as their mother when they are with us, yet they already have a mother—one who they clearly express their preference for everyday. Why do I bother? I thought this would be different. . . ."

Bio dad's take:

"Well, I have a wonderful new wife. Literally, she's *wonderful!* She'll be great with my kids; she takes care of everything the way I can't. She'll be just like the mom that they never had. This will be just like the family that I've always wanted. I've been given my second chance!"

These unrealistic expectations are common among newly divorced dads; they want to solve their immediate problem. No matter what, though, second families will never be or operate like the first family.

The kids' side of the story:

Children of divorce struggle with feelings of loss, guilt, and confusion, especially if their parents are fighting over them or one parent has recently been given limited or no custody. If Mom fights for or is given full custody—limiting their access to Dad—they may feel as though they have lost a parent. If Mom or Dad brings a new spouse into the family home and the kids are expected to bond with them immediately, this places them in unfamiliar territory. It also emphasizes the huge loss of having both biological parents in the family home.

Bio dad (without custody)'s thoughts:

From Dad's perspective, perhaps he has temporarily or permanently lost his rights to visitation or custody. For example, perhaps he's gone from seeing his children daily to seeing them four days per month (every other weekend). This loss can lead to feelings of guilt, anguish, isolation, and inferiority. Seeing his children every other weekend doesn't allow much time to influence the kids' upbringing. Losing custody means he has lost his opportunity to raise his children—one of the worst things a parent can experience. Making things more stressful, he usually has to financially support two households due to alimony and/or child support (instead of one household), which adds to increased feelings of losing control.

FOR EACH PERSON involved, positive and negative emotions influence their ability to make good decisions. Holding on to negative emotions, such as resentment, can make the situation toxic for everyone.

In the heat of the moment, adults often don't realize how their words and actions affect their kids. Once they move past this stage, they can see the devastating impact their fighting had on the kids.

Both parents love their children very much—if they didn't, there would not be this much emotion or conflict involved. However, the conflict is harmful to all involved. It is vital that you learn to set aside your emotions in order to make the best choices for yourself and your children.

Parents who are distracted by petty arguments often

make inappropriate and sometimes detrimental decisions out of anger, rage, resentment, and/or revenge. While you may be overly emotional in the present moment, if you do not learn how to manage your emotions, then you will negatively affect your kids no matter how hard you try to put them first. I can help you to identify, explore, and then effectively address the unrealistic versus realistic expectations you harbor.

Question #4: What Is Your Attitude Regarding the Situation?

Attribute #13: Realize Why This Situation Is Happening

What are you feeling? How intense are these feelings? Are these feelings dictating your words, actions, and life? If intense feelings are present, it means that you *care* about the situation. Now, let's do something about it.

When we look externally for people and things to blame, we get no further ahead. Instead of using this defense mechanism, let's look inside ourselves and address our positive and negative emotions, using them to fuel our motivation for change. Strong emotions means caring, and caring means potential for change.

Some people assume that men are less likely to care, perhaps because some men display indifference during a divorce. It's not that he doesn't care; he may simply act indifferent because he feels personal failure on some level. Perhaps he's too accommodating or he's avoiding the situation altogether. This is not evidence of uncaring.

Men and women deal with conflict differently. For instance, if a man goes hunting deer and he doesn't get the one he saw first, he simply moves on to the next one. After feeling defeated again and again by their ex-spouse or current wife (or whomever), men generally shut down and instead go after someone or something that's easier to deal with emotionally.

Ultimately, turning our attention inward gives us greater insight as to why a situation is unfolding the way it is. Even if you have a poor attitude to begin with, you can adjust it, because whether you know it or not, the feelings of love and commitment to your stepfamily are there.

Attribute #14: Understand the Detrimental Effects of Blame

Everyone has power, whether they know it or not; people often have trouble exercising it if they haven't learned the skill. Self-empowerment is integral to improving your internal self; this includes recognizing that you are not always right in every situation.

Do you have trouble admitting when you're wrong or have made a mistake? Self-empowerment also involves learning where your personal responsibilities lie. When are your words and actions contributing to a challenging situation?

The only person who you have control over is you. Regardless of the situation, your input can potentially change the situation or outcome in a positive or negative way. If all you add to the situation is negative input, you will only get a negative output from the situation.

Instead, you can overcome those negative emotions, harness their positive aspects, and reach those sometimes-hidden feelings of kindness and caring. Look deeply within and recognize whether you are blaming others instead of exploring how you can change the situation.

Attribute #15: How You Can Change the Outcome

Once you realize that you have the power to influence and control your actions and reactions, you will be empowered. It enables you to positively influence situations to increase the likelihood of your desirable outcomes. You can think of these as business managerial skills.

Dwelling in resentment harms you and those around you. Resentment prevents you from letting go of past hurts, moving past the conflict, and towards loving your blended family. To reverse the toxic effects engendered from resentment, let's recap: What's working in your life? What isn't? Next, create a list that addresses each of your issues (personal, familial, professional, or otherwise).

This isn't a simple to-do list; you'll want to include a column to record feelings and negative outcomes related to these issues. For example, perhaps you feel that you're expected to attend all of your stepkids' extracurricular events with both bio parents and a grand smile regardless of your wants and needs.

Step back to see the bigger picture. Where are these feelings coming from? Are you putting this guilt on yourself? Are you forcing yourself to be a super stepmother and to attend everything, only to result in building resentment over time? This resentment then leads to anger and rigidity in your relationship and parenting. Who does this help?

In another column or on another page, look at the situation as a whole. "The kids don't always ask me to attend. My husband wants me to know I'm welcome, but understands if I can't attend every event. Bio Mom probably wouldn't mind a break from my attendance. I could walk the dog during that time, which I love. . . ." As women and stepmothers, we put so much pressure on ourselves to be perfect that we often neglect the bigger picture.

Considering the bigger picture will clarify what the *real* problems are. Let's change or reframe the situation in a way that will empower us positively to make better decisions individually and for our blended family. Even the slightest shift in your perspective can have a positive impact on your situation's outcome.

Attribute #16: Learn to Take Personal Responsibility

Some things are so simple when we can step back and observe them. In the blended family, you are in the thick of it every minute of every day; it can be difficult to remain objective. Learning personal responsibility is incredibly empowering and stress-relieving.

What actions do you take when things aren't going your way? For example, if I wake up and I find the fridge isn't running properly, what do I do about it? I can ignore it and wait for my husband to fix it while all the food rots. I can blame him or the kids for not closing the door properly the night before resulting in electrical shortage. Or, I can fix it myself! Whether I call a repairman or check YouTube for a solution, I am perfectly capable of ensuring the fridge is running by the end of the day—and I feel better for it!

Try reframing your problems by adopting different perspectives. This ultimately gives you more control, and you will no longer feel dependent upon others. Many of these daily insignificant problems can be so easily fixed, giving you more energy and more positivity through your day. Taking initiative to solve your own problems can also improve your relationship.

Question #5: Are You Willing to Do What It Takes?

Attribute #17: Spreading the Joy Starts with You & Your Commitment

Like anything, if you're not committed, it's not going to work. Some people say, "Well, I am committed, but my husband is not committed." All you need is your own commitment, because that's what it takes to change your own outcomes—which will, in turn, then positively affect the rest of the family (unless your goal is to consume more wine).

Just one person's commitment to positive change sends positive waves throughout the house. If *you're* happier because *you* made changes in *your* personal life or behavior, it affects everybody. If you're suddenly smiling because you're happy (even when others aren't), then everyone else may start smiling with you—or they will want to know, "Why are you so happy? I want to smile, too."

Change has to start somewhere, and somebody must lead the charge; it might as well be you! Your commitment can shift your reality, which we will learn more about in the next attribute.

Attribute #18: Open Up to a New Reality

The next step is to open yourself to a new reality, a new way of being, and a new way of thinking. Doing so will empower you to become a leader as you regain your own strength and control over yourself.

A personal experience reflecting commitment to internal change and subsequent positive outcomes is as follows: I suffered a head injury in July 2013. I went from being the full-time caregiver at home to suddenly not being able to do anything; I couldn't work or be around the kids, and I had to sit in a dark room by myself for months.

That was the first time that I really faced the overall stepfamily situation and said, "This is not sustainable. If I don't do something now, this will fail." I've always been the type of person who doesn't rely on others to fix my problems. I try using my personal resources within myself and explore how I can change the situation, making it better for me, my husband, and my stepchildren.

Following my head injury, I started from the ground up. I was unable to cook dinner or do anything involving noise or lights. For the first time in my life, I had to listen to my body first, before the needs of those around me. Through commitment to myself, not my blended family, I took the time my body needed to heal instead of trying to be Super Stepmom.

One person's commitment to change will have a ripple effect through the whole family. When my stepdad first came into my mom's home, he realized my mom had not been parenting my siblings and I at all; we were wild! My stepdad totally changed our household. He came in committed and cared enough to turn our house into a home.

It took about three years. He taught us manners, how to cook and clean, how to cut the grass, and how to vacuum the pool. He remained committed and understood when we would say, "We want to go see our dad; he's more fun." But he never quit, he was committed to the blended family foundation that he had built in our home, he kept the rules that he made, and he followed through with the consequences. He was my mom's rock for many years, and he was our rock, too. What he did was very powerful, and even though we had a falling-out years later, I will never forget what he did for my siblings and I.

Attribute #19: Adopt New Behaviors & Attitudes

What is your ideal blended family scenario? Write it down. Study your list and recognize the various attributes and behaviors you've mentioned. Are *you* ready to behave this way? Are *you* ready to commit to this?

Decide what kind of stepmom you want to be, and then commit to becoming that ideal—adding a twist of your super personality. When you behave differently and express new positive attributes that you didn't know you had, everybody gets a better result.

If blended family dysfunction exists (which we will address later in this book), you will need to learn behaviors and interventions that will guide you in creating your ideal blended family situation. Some interventions and behaviors include household governance, respect, and role modeling for your stepchildren and their parents.

Adopt the attitude, "I will do this because it's good for me and my blended family." This attitude isn't easy to maintain. . . especially when things aren't going your way in this moment.

But imagine what it will be like 20 years from now when your children and/or stepchildren are in their early 20's and starting out on their own. You'll want to have modeled morals and behaviors that will guide them when they are testing the water without you.

If your goal is to see your children succeed (that's what we all want), then your focus needs to be on modeling and enforcing positive morals and behaviors at a young age; it's much easier for kids to learn good habits while they're young. It's difficult to hang on to that long-term view when you have challenging blended family dynamics at play, such as a bio dad who sees his kids only four days a month. This is why rewards reaped from goals met are so special.

Attribute #20: Your Reward Is Having a High-Functioning Blended Family

Congratulations! You are taking the first step in your blended family journey; you have been given a gift with the potential to become a better person and (step)mother and to touch the lives of each your family members.

This journey of personal and familial transformation is definitely not a quick fix; it will take commitment. Just as someone trying to lose 60 pounds doesn't expect the weight to disappear in three weeks, change takes time. You have to work hard, but it's absolutely worth it.

Element #2:

Fostering Relatability, a Sense of Compassion, & Empathy

This chapter focuses on the realization that showing compassion and empathy toward others involved in your blended family will always trump poor judgment and poor intentions.

Before we decided to tell my stepchildren about our new relationship, we did a lot of research. What I found is that no matter how much research you do, it will never unfold the way that you want or expect it to.

When we are in a challenging place, it is easy to look at the negative of our situation. We must challenge ourselves to see the positive aspects of every encounter in life. For some, this takes practice and a lot of brainstorming. That's okay!

Whenever we find ourselves stuck on the negatives, we tend to feed off this toxic mindset until it consumes every aspect of our lives. The danger of this is 1) self-sabotage, and 2) sabotaging the growth and development of your blended family by exposing them to such negative thinking.

Remember, kids will be watching and replicating everything you do. If either you or your husband give off negative energy consistently, the other is likely to follow suit—feeding from each other's negativity creates a downward spiral that is difficult to deviate from without conscious change.

When I talk about a person's "reality," I am referring to their cognitive thinking patterns, upbringing, life experiences, traditions, and all other factors contributing to what makes them tick as a person. Before I became truly compassionate about the realities of others, I was consistently judgmental and self-centered. In blended families, many identities and realities exist in the family unit, including 1) yours, 2) your husband's, 3) your identity as a couple, 4) your former spouse(s)', 5) each child's, 6) your husband's first family's, and so on. The amalgamation of these mindsets in the blended family can be incredible or detrimental, depending on how they are applied.

I'm sure you can think of a time when you judged a member of your blended family perhaps too harshly. How did it make you feel in the moment? How do you feel about it now? If you answered that you felt shame, anger, regret, or similar emotions, you are on track!

Ultimately, we all want what is best for each other. As parents and stepparents, we all have the same goals at the end of the day: we want our marriages to work, and we want our children to thrive and succeed. We may care for or love our children differently, at varying degrees, and with diverse goals for them. That's okay. Now we have to work together to reach those goals.

The takeaway message of this chapter is that by acknowledging and accepting the perspectives of others, it becomes easier to be compassionate. When you're compassionate, you judge less and you care more. When you care more, everything runs a lot smoother, and you're happier with yourself at the end of the day.

Question #6: What Is Your Current Reality Like?

Attribute #21: Your Roles & Responsibilities in Your Blended Family

How do you belong in your family? Do you feel as though you even have an established role? What does being a stepmom mean to you? Society has defined expectations of what moms and dads are supposed to adhere to. What about stepparents? There really is no set definition. You may find it helpful to note what you *think* your role is (or should be), from which we can work to build a strong stepmother persona for you.

Not knowing your role and expectations within your blended family adds to your uncertainty and anxiety. While adult, you may be feeling some degree of discomfort when trying to find your place. You can imagine how difficult it is for the children, whose feelings of anxiety are magnified. Their feelings are often more intense and difficult to cope with because children lack the coping skills that an adult has (hopefully) acquired.

In addition to contemplating your own role in your family, you should also consider how you can provide a sense of belonging for your stepchildren. When they don't know what is expected of them or what will happen next in their new family, they need extra security. Security can be present in the forms of family structure, household structure, and a sense of belonging.

Attribute #22: How You Feel about the Role You Play

You can either define your role or you cannot. If you don't know what your role entails (most stepparents don't), you don't know what to expect. Children who haven't been given rules and expectations from which to live by are more uncertain of their world. They are constantly guessing what their parents expect of them. To empathize, let's consider a person in a new job who has not been given any training. They don't know what to do and are trying anything and everything to gain their boss's approval to prevent themselves from getting fired.

This is a high-stress situation, even for an adult. The adult needs the job for growth and survival, just like the child needs their parent's acceptance for growth and survival. Add the stress of moving from house to house, living with different sets of parents and expectations (or no expectations), and you can see how this is a recipe for the erosion of your stepchild's confidence and self-worth.

Even when we know what is expected of us, we also know how it feels to have a big change occur in our lives. At first, we may be resistant to change, leading to feelings of resentment. If you don't provide the support your stepchildren need, they can start to feel lost and withdraw. Are you truly comfortable with this role you must provide? It is natural to harbor anger towards this role, but we can work through this.

To ensure that you are meeting their needs, you need to clearly establish and communicate your role in the family, as well as their roles. By sharing with them what each of your family responsibilities are, it will be easier for your stepchildren to understand and accept their own age-appropriate responsibilities.

Whether resentment or other strong emotions are present, you must learn and teach your family to normalize their emotions and express them in a healthy way. This is why having family structure and role expectations are so beneficial; without expectations, nobody knows what anybody else needs from them. Knowing what is expected of you provides security and encourages you to act accordingly.

Attribute #23: Understand How Loyalty Binds Work in Your Blended Family

A loyalty bind is an emotional connection where the loyalty is tied. This is another challenging aspect of blended families. A child's loyalty often remains with both of their biological parents after divorce, but now they are no longer with both parents in the same household. During the divorce crisis, parents are usually very angry with each other. Oftentimes, Mom spends the most time with the children, and—without realizing it—ends up using the child as an emotional crutch.

When parents bad-mouth each other in front of or to the children, whether through words or body language, the child will pick up on that. If the child begins to believe that Dad is not worthy in Mom's eyes, then that child automatically believes that they *themselves* are not worthy. Remember, the child is naturally half of each parent, and that's how they define themselves. The child will defend both parents, but ultimately, the loyalty will remain with the parents who they spend the most time with—simply for survival.

Children will often side with the biological parent who is *not* present and try to keep the loyalty known there. For example, if they are with Dad and Stepmom, they may say things like, "Mom's lasagna is better." They are simply trying to express their loyalty that remains with Mom. Stepmom must learn that this isn't personal; it means that they are confused about who the new person in their lives is and how they are supposed to react to them.

Loyalty binds are situational and environmental, so with each change of the environment, loyalty binds may shift. If the kids are with Dad, often, the loyalty bind is with their mom because Mom is not present; they need to preserve her memory. On the other hand, when they are with Mom, the psychological loyalty remains with Dad because Dad is not there. However, concurrently, they must show their loyalty to Mom for survival.

A sense of loyalty can be very confusing for children of blended families. In their minds, conflict exists between whom they are *supposed* to be loyal to at any given time. This will wear on them mentally if unaddressed, leading to low self-esteem, reduced confidence, low self-worth, and increasing resentment, guilt, and shame. Kids will often target the stepparent because they have no loyalty ties yet.

Attribute #24: Stop Playing the Victim

Emotions and personal beliefs are often suppressed by each member of the blended family. When you are feeling resentment, it is up to you to take charge and change the situation; children do not have this capability. We, as adults, must learn to stop blaming and feeling sorry for ourselves. By stepping outside of our emotions, we can then make wise decisions for all children involved. Adult decisions are for the adults to make. These decisions are a prerequisite to children maintaining a level of normalcy in this new family situation. Let's work at transforming your current reality into a positive one!

Question #7: What Are the Realities of Others in Your Family Like?

Now we are going to shift from the role or reality that you experience, to your perceptions of the role or reality of others in your blended family experience.

Attribute #25: Realize Where Unhelpful Entitlement & Selfishness Originate

This can go both ways. If you are in a highly conflictual situation and you're just trying to survive the day, an element of entitlement and selfishness will be present. Entitlement and selfishness may be necessary to meet our needs sometimes, but this attitude become unhelpful when we neglect the needs of others.

For Stepmom, it's very easy to resort to judgment. For example, a stepmom may be thinking, "These kids are so entitled! All they think about is themselves. They don't care about what makes their dad or me happy." Of course they don't—they're kids. What makes this blended family dynamic challenging is that Stepmom shares no DNA with her stepchildren, and therefore naturally has less tolerance and empathy for them.

But what if Stepmom could experience what others in her blended family were going through? Would she have more compassion and empathy? Would she be more tolerant and show more caring?

In life, we all see others from our own perspective and project our reality onto others. We each have our own reality that we work to build and defend. When we feel that our reality is threatened, we tend to care about ourselves first, which can lead to selfishness and entitlement. Imagine if you could learn another way—how to empathize with others instead of only seeing things your way. How much would this change every interaction in your life?

Attribute #26: Let Go of Defensiveness & Conflict

Defensiveness and conflict originate from protecting your reality. In the blended family, when we are each fighting for our own reality and not considering others, conflict arises from every angle. We are all guilty of wishing others would behave a certain way to make us happy. Remember that old saying: "You can't change anyone but yourself"? It applies here, too. You simply cannot force a person to behave a certain way to make you happy. If, instead, we learned to understand the motivation behind their behavior, we would become more compassionate toward their stance.

Between blended family households, conflict often exists. Each bio parent wants to provide their child the perfect life at their house, and often, they aim to outshine the other parent. Yet in this scenario, while they're fighting to be the better parent, they are losing the opportunity to be a real, normal parent. Constant competition leaves them stressed and on the edge, which reduces their ability to raise their children.

Attribute #27: Address "Our House Is *Perfect,* but the Other House. . ." Thinking

It is very easy to *assume* that your house is the better rearing environment of the two blended family homes. The truth is that we all come to the table with vastly different experiences and skill sets. *Nobody's perfect.* It is unfair to suggest that one household is worse than the other in terms of raising the children "properly" (unless evidence of physical or emotional abuse exists; this is different and should be dealt with immediately). In most cases, there are two parents who absolutely love their children, want to be with their children, and are trying to make the best of an undesirable situation.

The ultimate reality is that the governance of the other household is no longer your business (except when ensuring the safety of your child); this came with your decision to divorce and live *separate* lives. If you are super parents and develop a co-parenting plan, both agreeing to X, Y, and Z for the children, then the other household is *somewhat* your business. Good boundary creation and respect for the boundaries of others are imperative in the blended family situation. When you drop the kids off at the other house, you must learn to walk away and trust that the other parent will do what they have agreed. In turn, they will trust you when you have the kids at your home.

Attribute #28: Honor the Realities of Others

If you don't respect each person's reality and their different skills and experiences, you will never find harmony. Just because you accept a person's reality does not mean you agree with their behavior.

A crucial part of becoming an empathetic, empowered adult is accepting the realities of others and truly believing, "This is who that person is. Their reality is as important as mine in this situation. Our marriage to each other has ended, but I respect who they are and know they love our child as much as I do, regardless of their behavior moving forward."

The solution comes from learning how to accept, let go, and step back from the other household. You can do this by focusing on your own household instead and how you may improve it. Every single person in this world has a different reality that you will never experience. If you can accept the reality of a dear friend (even though they do certain things that you wish they wouldn't do) because you're friends, then you know you can have the same acceptance here with your husband's former spouse.

Sometimes, I comically remind myself, "I'm not married to her; I'm married to him. Therefore, what she does is actually none of my business. If it was supposed to be my business, I would have been married to her instead."

You don't have to be friends with your partner's ex-spouse, but you do have to honor their reality. In their reality, perhaps they truly believe that they are the superior parent in the equation. Regardless of their reality, this is your journey to becoming an empathic, empowered adult. Let's face it: There is nothing you can do about what goes on in their head. They will not change their way of thinking just because it upsets you. Acceptance will bring you freedom from further conflict and allow you to release any resentment you are harboring.

Question #8: What If You Discovered What Was Really True for Your Family?

Attribute #29: Acknowledge That We Are All Experiencing Change, Loss, & Grief

Everybody deals with change differently. You might have one child who is totally withdrawn, in their room all the time with the door closed and their headphones on. You might have another child who is acting out, crying or screaming more than usual, and needing extra attention. We know there are differences in the way each person reacts to loss and grief. In adults, symptoms of grief may be more subtle and difficult to spot, but it is there.

We must learn to empathize with others. If are lashing out or are at the hands of someone who is lashing out, that adds to the stress of your own grief. Remember that others may not deal with grief the same way as you do (or the way you would like), this does not make them a bad person. Take the time to consider factors contributing to their grief. Empathize with them. Whether it's you, your husband, his ex, the children; you will feel empowered by being considerate.

Attribute #30: Create Harmony through Compromise

In all blended family roles, as in all relationships, compromise exists. One of the main challenges of a blended family is the loss of the "ideal" nuclear family. For example, the child now has to live with only one of their biological parents, not two. That's a compromise. Now they also potentially have to share a room with a child who is not even their biological brother or sister.

A soon-to-be stepmom who is marrying a man who decides he doesn't want any more children because he already has two or three from a previous marriage: that's a compromise. From every angle in the blended family comes compromise. This can erode your desire to be in a blended family, as well as your work towards harmony and peace. It's difficult to continue giving when you sincerely feel that you aren't getting in return.

On the other hand, you have been given a gift to become a better person (and a better adult) by learning the art of compromising. That lets you create harmony in your blended family and marriage, which will improve all your relationships throughout your life.

Attribute #31: The Solution to Thinking, "Help! I Always Come Second. . ."

As a stepmom, you may notice a pattern where you are not number one the way you might have been in a first marriage without existing children. Everything seems second-best. You're the second wife. You're the stepmom, which means you're the "second" or "backup" mom.

Seemingly, everyone and everything has precedence over you. If, however, you can learn to accept this for what it factually is instead of taking it personally, you will find peace within. Fine-tuning your expectations can allow you to find happiness within yourself and with the situation. When you reach this space of acceptance, you will attain a new level of your authentic self.

Attribute #32: Recognize That This Way is Empowering!

You can become your happiest self by modifying your personal expectations to become more realistic to the situation. If, within the first six months, you expect your stepchildren to tell you they love you before they go to bed, you are likely to feel a sense of failure when it doesn't happen. Instead, you might enjoy "Good morning" greetings from them. If this is your goal, start to model the behavior for them without feeling crushed if the gesture isn't reciprocal at first. Eventually, they will follow suit if they feel safe, unthreatened, and unpressured.

We all have to start somewhere; we cannot expect everyone to respond and react the way *we* want, especially emotionally wounded people. You have to commit to working at it. Though you entered this situation with a set of your own expectations, you will find that you are truly building relationships from the ground up—with some people who may not desire a relationship with you at all. Ultimately, your expectations must suit the situation and goals; your stepchildren may not love you right away, but you can model politeness and appropriate behavior.

Question #9: What If You Adopted a New Perception?

You cannot change people; you can only change yourself, and nobody is coming to save you. This means you must truly look within to find out what personal wounds need healing and/or modification.

What are your triggers? Let's identify them and dig deep to excavate the unnecessary baggage your carrying. This will make you lighter and happier! It all begins with adjusting your attitude about yourself and your family. Your attitude shift will affect your actions and reactions, which will create a ripple effect throughout your life.

Attribute #33: End the "Denial & Blame" Game

Imagine for a moment that you no longer blamed anyone in this world for *your* issues. Imagine you could not deny your own feelings and reactions anymore.

What if you learned to accept you for *you*? How would that feel? What would it be like to release your emotional barriers to happiness? Freedom from guilt, blame, and shame will relieve the heaviness resting on your shoulders and chest, the constant uneasy feeling in your stomach, and the actual excess weight you are carrying on your body. When those negative emotions are no longer holding you hostage, you can start seeing the bigger, beautiful picture.

When I first became a stepmother, I gained 15 pounds in the first six months. I had never carried extra weight on my 5' 2" body frame before. Determined to prove I would be a great stepmother and second wife, I put the needs of my blended family first (even my extended blended family). However, what I reached was my personal detriment.

When I began accepting myself and my feelings from the inside out, and I began taking care of *me*, the emotional, psychological, and physical weight began to disappear. A good maintenance will keep you and your body in check.

The best way to work with your strong emotions and/or unhealthy beliefs is by focusing on your desired outcome. This way, we can break down your immediate problems so they seem smaller and are easier to handle. For instance, when I experience an adverse outcome, I reground myself by re-establishing *my* ultimate goals. If I have a disagreement with my husband, I retell my brain *our* ultimate goals. I remind myself that he is on *my* team and that our actions and reactions are coming from a loving willingness to reach our goals together. We have common objectives; knowing this helps me to listen to him rather than attacking his position or becoming defensive.

Likewise, you can work with your partner to truly hear what they are saying, instead of taking offense at any little thing that contradicts what you expect or believe to be true. Learning to heal and express your emotions of resentment, blame, or guilt in a healthy way provides you extra emotional room to experience peace, harmony, understanding, and empathy.

Attribute #34: Envision Co-Parenting without Negative Emotions

As you learn to accept and release feelings of guilt and shame, you are providing your body-mind room for growth and good feelings. It's like pruning a bush or trimming those split ends that prevent your hair from healthy growth. Happiness and contentment will improve your relationships with yourself, your partner, and everyone around you.

Next, you can learn to accept and release emotions arising from the co-parenting process. When this internal shift occurs, suddenly the repercussions of the other household's choices don't affect you the way they did before.

For example, if you realize the drop-off process (where Mom drops the kids off at your place for visitation) is a trigger for you because it evolves into a grand theatre production of hugs, tears, and tantrums, trial-offer to pick them up instead. This alters the environment and creates a fresh slate to create new habits and routines with the kids. It's also empowering to take responsibility and rebalance the situation. You may not realize it, but you might also be doing your ex-spouse and children a favor; perhaps Mom has trouble saying goodbye to her babies and subconsciously adds to the drama without wanting to.

Proactively taking control of your own happiness and goals, along with doing what it takes to make yourself feel good, will result in less stress, more energy, and greater self-esteem and self-worth.

Attribute #35: Recognize Efforts of Others by Considering Their Perspective

Another core quality you can develop that will bring you inner peace is learning to put yourself in the shoes of your family members. For example, if you're a new step-mom to an 8-year-old girl, you can put yourself in her shoes to explore alternate reasons for her highly emotive outbursts or inappropriate behavior. Why might she be reacting this way? How would the 8-year-old you feel and respond if your parents had recently divorced, you were forced to change schools and change homes, you could no longer have both your parents all the time, and you had to *welcome* a new stepmother figure into your home?

Behavioral reactions of others in your life can be dealt with similarly. Before you react to someone's inappropriate behavior, do you stop to consider what they might be going through in their personal lives? Perhaps you feel your husband's ex-wife is not the easiest person to get along with, but between feeling heartbreak over her failed marriage (even if she no longer wants him) and subsequently believing that she's been "replaced" by you, she may not be operating as her greatest self.

Learning to experience empathy for others becomes easier when you can see the situation from their point of view and realize what factors may be contributing to their way of thinking. Being able to acknowledge what others are going through in any facet of life allows you to recognize that they may truly be doing their best with the resources that they have, and forgive.

Attribute #36: Perceive Others from Their Highest Standard

What happens when we change our expectations for everyone involved? What happens if, for a short while, we let go of our expectations of others or of events, and just see what happens? Releasing stringent expectations gives others the space they may need to show up as their best self. If we did that, who knows what's possible—and you won't be wasting your energy *telling* people (aggressively or passive-aggressively) how things *should* be done according to you. This gives you and them greater freedom; you are free to focus on how *you* can interact with them positively, and they are free to do their best instead of fearing judgement from you.

Question #10: How Can You Learn to Experience Another's Reality through Compassionate Eyes?

Attribute #37: See That Everyone Is Entitled to Their Own Perception of Reality

Part of showing compassion for others is accepting them for who they are regardless of their reality. Focus on living your own life fuller, greater, and happier, rather than judging others and telling them what you think they *should* be doing. Once you can step back and let others take control of their own lives, you will see favorable results (though maybe not at first).

Everyone comes to the table with their own experiences, skill sets, and mind; everyone has a right to their own thoughts, feelings, beliefs, and methods. Accepting that allows you to move forward and act in a more kind and loving manner toward yourself and others.

Attribute #38: Honor Other People's Right to Their Own Reality

Personal growth begins with realizing you need to shift your focus from the external (trying to "fix" other people's behavior or lifestyle) to the internal (improving your own behavior or lifestyle). Remind yourself that we all come from various backgrounds, including level of education, beliefs and experiences in family health, work history, relationships with others, and our relationship with ourselves. We are all different, and that's a blessing! Ultimately, we don't have control over anyone else's actions or thoughts, but our own.

The good news: You don't need to control others to get the results you want! Celebrating diversity among the members within your blended family can truly have advantages. In our home, each adult and child has distinct skills and life experiences that they bring to the table. We can learn about life, commitment, cooperation, and, most of all, about ourselves in a blended family.

Attribute #39: Don't Take It Personally

Consistently taking things personally (especially things out of your control) inhibits your personal growth, and prevents you from honoring the realities of others. An exercise I practice is to think back to a personal event where I took something personally (perhaps I missed the net when one more goal could have won us the game), and then analyze how the situation may have turned out differently had I refused to take it personally. Would I have been so hard on myself later in life when I missed an accomplishment?

If you can learn to stop taking things personally, you will have the space to see the bigger picture. You will realize that others are not necessarily acting and reacting because they are against you; they may be battling a completely separate issue altogether of which you know nothing. There could be ten other reasons, none of them involving you.

By appreciating that the actions of others are out of your control, you come into your own power. You have the power to respond in a more positive light despite their negativity, which brings a better outcomes for everyone.

Attribute #40: Take Responsibility for the Things You Can Change

The only person that you can change is yourself. If you keep that idea in the back of your mind, it will turn into a personal belief and allow you to actually take more responsibility for your own personal happiness instead of relying on the actions and reactions of others. Ultimately, the only person who can make you happy is you.

Element #3:
Adopting Planning & Communication Skills That Make Blended Families Work

A strong foundational family system must be in place for smooth operation within and between households. Good communication, especially with your partner, is vital to the strength of your family's foundation.

When we first brought our new blended family together, my husband and I were not consulting each other regularly before giving permission to our girls. Using an unstructured approach to parenting was ineffective. Our girls would ask Dad or me for permission for things based on who was more likely to say yes.

One Saturday, we had movie tickets for a 4 p.m. show for the four of us. Just as we were about to leave, three little girls showed up for a sleepover—Dad had forgotten he had invited them a week ago. During the sleepover, a colleague showed up with her kids for a barbecue that they had been "invited" to by my generous husband. Unprepared for all of this, I raced to the grocery store before our guests could see me sweat.

Any successful relationship or family needs effective communication. Since then, we consult with each other before inviting guests over or giving the kids permission for activities or events. The first answer we always give the kids is, "We will discuss this soon and get back to you."

Question #11: How Do You Feel About Rules & Governance in Your Family?

Attribute #41: Accept That Your Blended Family Was Not Planned

Unlike a first family, which had the opportunity to grow together, there is often little or no planning in this second family. Perhaps you assumed it would be just like your first family—or even easier, but with a few different players.

When a family is forced together haphazardly and no plan is in place, it's very different than a first family. In a blended family, there is no foundational structure in place: no blueprint, no rules, and no governance. There are all of these new people in a new household, and neither you nor anybody else really knows what is expected of you or of them.

Instead of relying on the assumption that your new family will work like your first family did, you must accept that the two are completely different and need to be cared for differently. Most people unknowingly have the same expectations for their blended family as they had for their first family, and subsequently act on those beliefs. This can be detrimental to all involved. It leads to chronic feelings of personal unmet expectations, which then leads to decreased self-esteem, self-worth, confidence, and self-love.

As a stepmother, you may enter a new blended family marriage truly believing, "I love my new husband, so I'll naturally love his kids." How badly do you feel about yourself when it doesn't happen this easily? You begin to doubt yourself: "Is the problem with me or with them?"

I'm happy to announce that neither of you are to blame; this dynamic is normal and can be managed effectively. It's time to look at your blended family with a new lens. You can accept that your second family is different from a first family, and still find true happiness.

Attribute #42: Learn Why a Foundation in Blended Families Matters

When the blended family lacks structure, authority and respect break down: members don't know what is expected of them or how they are supposed to behave or react. This is especially true of children who are bouncing back and forth between two houses, since the two sets of adults might have two very different ways of doing things in their respective homes.

Within the home of stepmom and dad, she may feel the kids behave inappropriately when they want something and need more guidance; perhaps that behaviour is the only behavior Dad knows because that's the way it was in their old house. This signals that Dad and Stepmom need to backtrack and set up *new* rules and *new* goals within the *new* family.

As a stepmom, on one hand you're trying to build an alliance between you and the kids, or at the very least building an amicable relationship where they don't hate everything you symbolize; on the other hand, you are an authority figure and leader in the home (especially with stepchildren of the same sex) and must often stand your ground. This can be extremely difficult when you and your partner work full time, your kids are enrolled in many activities, and you are simply exhausted. Probably the last thing you feel like doing is addressing a sensitive issue that might be perceived by your husband or stepchild as negative or against them. In the long run, if these issues are not confronted, it can be damaging to the relationships.

When our lives become overly busy and stress brews, discipline is often the first element of household regulation to go. We may avoid disciplining either for fear of ruffling feathers, or because we simply cannot handle any more added stress. You may refrain from disciplining because you don't want to be ostracized by the children or your partner in case they disagree with your decision. Your husband may let up on discipline because he is uncertain of the outcome; perhaps he is worried the children will choose not to return to his home if he is too strict. (Notice how in both scenarios the parents are making decisions based on their feelings of discomfort and not necessarily what's best for the children.)

You may be wondering if it is the stepmother's role to discipline at all. From my perspective, it truly depends on the parenting plan you and your partner have decided on. Disciplining stepchildren is a sensitive subject and requires careful planning and execution to be successful.

Attribute #43: Realize That Avoiding Household Regulation Does Not Help

By avoiding discipline in the home for fear of an undesirable outcome or uncomfortable personal feelings, we are ultimately failing as parents. Our responsibility is to prepare our children by exercising their internal and external resources so they can learn to love themselves, enjoy happiness, and live a good life.

In the context of a blended family, it is imperative that a parenting and co-parenting plan be in place for the children to continue to grow and develop naturally as if a divorce had not happened. Teaching good morals, personal responsibility, and self-care has to start at an early age (or as soon as the blended family comes together).

If you do not currently have a parenting plan in your blended family, that could be a main cause of chaos. The good news is it is never too late to create and implement an effective parenting plan, but it will take commitment and patience to follow through.

Attribute #44: Introduce Governance & Order to Your Blended Family

Just as a business has a structure that ensures each person within the organization knows what their job is and how to do it, a family also needs structure to feel belonging. Take a moment to examine your current family structure.

How are goals accomplished? How are day-to-day household tasks completed? What activities or rules encourage cohesiveness and a sense of belonging? Are you happy with the current family structure? How do your family members feel about it?

Harmony and belonging won't exist if you don't have the right structure in place that is unique to your family. When people's homes are in chaos, their personal lives are likely to be overburdened with unnecessary stress on their bodies and minds. Children and adults alike thrive with structure, which gives them order, balance, safety, and a sense of security.

It's challenging to establish new structure where no structure has previously existed. It will take time and patience, but it is absolutely worth it when you give your family the gift of stability and security in an uncertain situation. Life becomes more enjoyable, and everyone can relax when they know what is expected of them.

When more change occurs in the blended family, every day is a challenge, especially in the first few months of implementing the new structure. After that, it becomes second nature for everyone involved. Even if you are the sole family member committed to change, you can make a remarkable difference. Your new attitude will have a profound effect on you, your love for yourself, and will create a ripple effect on those around you.

Question #12: What Is Your Family Hierarchy?

Attribute #45: Develop a Foundation Together

The foundation of your family structure is the relationship that you have with your husband. By finding out exactly what you expect of each other and where your relationship needs love and nurturing, you can learn to work better together as a team. From your strong foundation, you will build on your platform pillars that each member can lean on daily for love and security.

Attribute #46: Create a Co-Parenting Plan

You and your husband can create a written agreement discussing what each of your roles and responsibilities are within your home, followed by a co-parenting plan with your husband's former spouse. By creating this co-parenting plan, you can define rules, regulations, roles, and responsibilities to migrate everyone onto the same page. This allows for positive collaboration—working with each other, not against each other.

Let's say you have a preference about which days the kids are with you throughout the week. If you have an open platform established from which you can discuss this, you may find it easier to reach an agreement. For example, instead of arguing about who gets the kids for the 4th of July on the 3rd, you will have already planned and agreed on visitation dates. Remember, a lack of a defined schedule makes children feel insecure and uncertain; your arguing over them makes these feelings worse.

A co-parenting plan does not mean that you get to start setting rules for how the kids will live in the other house; that is up to their mom and stepdad, not you and your husband. Each house is its own entity with its own rules, and the children will learn which rules they need to follow in which house.

The co-parenting plan is created to help identify common goals, methods, and support to create the best environments. For example, if your child has been doing poorly in math, a common goal in the co-parenting plan might be to practice math problems for 15 minutes each night.

At your house, it might happen at 4 p.m.; at Mom's, it might happen after dinner. The small details don't matter; the overall commitment to the goal does.

The most important tool making co-parenting *easier* is this co-parenting plan; a blended family without a plan will fall apart. With a structural foundation between you and your husband, a co-parenting plan in place, and an empowering attitude, your blended family now has the basic tools to thrive.

Attribute #47: Your Co-Parenting Agreement & Follow Through

While you are establishing your set of roles, responsibilities, and rules for your house with your husband, the other household should do the same. There is also a third set of rules: the co-parenting agreement, which outlines common goals, paths, parental roles, and responsibilities. Commitment is what makes this new structure work, which is why all adults should sign the agreement if possible.

As you build a strong structure for your family, remember to set long-term goals as well as short-term and intermediate goals. For example, your long-term goal might be that your 15-year-old stepson graduates from high school with sufficient grades and a healthy body and mind. If this is your goal, then a plan should be in place to help him achieve this. Perhaps you encourage him to become involved in a team sport to develop team-building skills, or you help him create a study space and schedule to help him learn how, when, and why studying is important.

When you and your husband create your home parenting plan together, be creative; reach for the stars but also maintain realistic expectations of everyone involved.

Numerous studies demonstrate that children are less likely to succeed in a household without governance, rules, and expectations. The subsequent outcome of healthy home boundaries, roles, and expectations are self-worth, respect, love, and appreciation. These outcomes may not be evident overnight; it takes time and patience.

Having household governance does not mean becoming a drill sergeant type to help your kids to succeed in school and in life. Having sensible, relevant rules and expectations can make all the difference and support family identity and a sense of belonging. Giving your child healthy boundaries fosters greater independence and, thus, self-confidence.

If we neglect giving our children the appropriate expectations, they feel less secure, have less confidence, and feel more like a visitor in your home than a family member who belongs. Allow your children to take part in the governance planning process. Ask them what they think good rules are for themselves (or what rules they would make if they were the parents), and then fill in any gaps (often, their set consequences are much worse than ours).

What happens when the other household refuses to participate in a co-parenting plan? Firstly, I must say that when this occurs, the only ones paying for this mistake are, unfortunately, the children. However, if this happens, it is not the end. Remember from earlier, we can only change or have control over ourselves. Instead, put all your energy into making your children feel loved in your home so they can continue to grow in a secure, stable, predictable environment. You cannot control what happens at the other home. You have been awarded shared custody (or whatever your case scenario may be); therefore, you must trust that the other parent loves the children, too, even if it isn't done your way.

Establishing rules and expectations for your household does not have to be a negative thing. Why not create rewards for good behavior (such as letting your 17-year-old stepson borrow the car twice a week if he maintains a certain GPA). You can also schedule fun weekly/biweekly family meetings to discuss what's working and what's not, brainstorm solutions, and finish with a fun game you all enjoy.

Remember to comment on both the small and significant accomplishments of your children; find out what is important to them. What are their personal goals? Help them reach them!

Can you see where I'm going with this? This can be a creative and fun process that will help you to calm nerves, get necessary tasks done, and enjoy a sense of belonging in your blended family's home.

Attribute #48: Establish a Blended Family Culture

A way to establish favorable culture within your family and home is through your family governance structure that you have created. What do the two of you value? What do you want to pass on to your children? Respect? Tidiness? Punctuality?

Relying on the rules and expectations that you created can give children the structure to attain these goals. However, if you set the rules, you must follow them, too, for mutual respect and appreciation. For example, if you would like to be consulted before the children invite guests over, the family "rule" may entail this response to their request: "Let me get back to you on that. I'll check with Dad first," instead of giving them permission without consulting your husband.

We know that by human nature, children can be manipulative when they want something. This happens in first families, too. In the blended family, this issue is of particular relevance because the children are constantly testing their stability and security after divorce. Show unity with your partner, and be committed to saying what you mean and meaning what you say. Never give in to your child without first discussing the issue with your partner. Show them lots of love, and reassure them that they will get an answer soon enough. By showing unity, you reassure the children of the strong foundation between you and your husband so they can feel safe and secure, knowing what to expect.

After a child's parents divorce, their safety and psychological security are compromised. In order to prove that it can be restored and present in their new family, you must show that you are strong and that no matter how much they question or protest, you will adhere to the expectations and rules created for the family. When the foundation of a structure sticks together, it allows the building's strength to shine. With proper care and maintenance, it will last.

Question #13: Is Healthy Communication Flowing?

Attribute #49: Encourage Communication between Households

The next aspect of a healthy blended family is healthy communication. How are you communicating between households? The biggest no-no is communicating through your children instead of directly with each other, which is a trap that many blended families fall into. Parents are so angry and hurt that they cannot stand to talk to each other, and they end up sending messages through the children.

This behavior is really stressful for children; it may not appear to stress them, but ultimately, you are expecting your children to handle adult issues. For example, if Dad tells the children to give Mom a message, that adds adult responsibilities onto the child. The child may accidentally forget, or they may not want to upset Mom. Instead, send an email, text, or leave a quick phone message. This prevents your children from having to be "adults" in an already chaotic, back-and-forth home situation.

If you have been using your kids as couriers between you and other adults who you dislike talking to, it is time to stop. Rely on a different form of communication instead.

Which form of communication would work the best for you and the other adults involved? Is it email, a phone call, or a weekly in-person meeting? Establish a good mode of communication among the adults, and determine the ideal frequency of communication so that none of you miss out on important information about what is happening with the kids. At my home, we use email and text, and we "cc" (carbon copy) each other on everything, from teachers to sports coaches to appointments and more. It works well!

Attribute #50: Take Raw Emotion out of the Communication & Decision-Making Process

One of the most difficult skills to learn is setting aside your emotions. It does not mean ignoring or neglecting your emotions; it means putting them on the shelf until the appropriate time comes to work through them and heal.

Setting aside your emotions is a skill worth learning:

your children (and everyone you interact with) will benefit from you using this skill during a conflict or during decision-making. Try filtering your negative mental energy to allow yourself to view situations differently; for example, if your mind is in negative energy and you believe an ex-spouse is trying to purposely sabotage you, you may need to reset your energy before judging their actions.

Don't believe that others in your blended family unit are trying to sabotage you (even if they are); instead, view their hurt without taking it personally. It is really easy to blame your new stepchildren when you are having problems in your new marriage. However, it is rarely the children's fault; the problems occurring arise from a lack of a good foundation in your relationship with your husband.

Let go of the negativity preventing you from accepting the true reality of the situation—the bigger picture—setting aside strong toxic emotions before making important decisions. There is always a time and a place to deal with these strong emotions: away from the children, in a safe environment.

Attribute #51: Reach an Agreement on Blended Family Operation

Sit down with your spouse and then your children to create a family plan that works for everyone. You can't expect to please everyone, but having some compromise is part of working together as a family and a team. You can be extremely happy with the success of the plan, but the main goal of the plan is to help you be a healthy, well-managed family.

Keep in mind while creating this plan and your set of family rules that you cannot let *your* feelings of guilt about the divorce dictate the way you parent your children (by becoming a push-over parent, *laissez-faire* parent, or "*democratic*" parent).

Also important here: material things and expensive outings will never outweigh simple family closeness and the joy of just *being* together. Through my program, we will work together to establish a family plan, rules, and a joint family calendar, among other beneficial elements.

Attribute #52: Create an Accountability System

Now that you have established your plan as a family, a mechanism must be introduced to hold each member accountable. Set up a system where family members can be accountable so that the processes works like a well-oiled machine. A time investment is required here in the beginning, but it will yield more time and energy for all in the long run.

It can be more challenging for a biological mom to commit to regular discipline than it is for a biological dad. Often, the disciplining process is straightforward overall for a man, unless he's parenting from guilt and avoids discipline altogether during the four days a month he has visitation. For a woman, discipline can seem like a confusing open dialogue constantly running in her head: "Okay, should I say something now? Or should I just let it go? Should I fight this battle, or should I try to win this war?" Having a family plan in place automatically answers these questions for you, freeing up head space for more important things.

Ultimately, you should be able to have an open dialogue with your partner about maintaining the process by making people accountable. We built a strong foundation earlier to be able to let each other know when we need some backup in the discipline department.

Question #14: What Are Your Family's Rules, Responsibilities, & Expectations?

Attribute #53: Eliminate Miscommunication & Misperception

Through this strategy, you are creating roles, responsibilities, and realistic expectations for each member of your blended family. Everyone should understand exactly what their role is and what is expected of them. For example, perhaps every Monday, it has been established that Johnny will walk the family dog. In order to maintain this expectation, his "chores" should be in writing and fully understood. Getting Johnny to initial his chore after completion will teach him accountability. Perhaps you give him $2 every week when all his chores have been completed as reward.

Outlining expectations and having family meetings may seem like a lot of work, but it will actually save you more time and energy overall. It eliminates miscommunication and prevents members from sabotaging rules. The roles and expectations are written down instead of "verbalized" or "remembered," which helps to prevent future arguments and uncertainty.

When you know what is expected of you, that certainty eliminates doubt, allowing you to feel more secure in your stable environment. Children need this feeling of security, especially after their parents' divorce. Using this method for family planning and regulation simplifies tasks and goals. Instead of constantly wondering whether you should do something or not, there is an established structure to follow. Having children adhere to the structure teaches responsibility and accountability, but also makes them feel loved and gives them a sense of belonging. As the stepmom, your roles, responsibilities, and expectations also become more clearly defined.

Attribute #54: See the Importance of *Clearly* Established Rules & Expectations

When you lack rules and clear expectations, your children won't understand why you are upset after they did something, because they won't know *why* they failed to meet your expectations. If your boss is not monitoring your progress or you don't know what your boss expects of you at work, it is very easy to sabotage your role, manipulate certain things, and get away with other things.

On the other hand, if your boss neglects to monitor your progress and then fires you for no apparent reason, you feel awful. We don't want our children to feel this way. We want to establish clear roles, expectations, and boundaries so they don't grow up worrying about pleasing us. Unclear roles lead to miscommunication and misinterpretation of important messages.

Establishing roles and responsibilities with children teaches them about the relationship between cause and effect. If you complete the task you were supposed to, you will be rewarded; if you don't, there will be consequences. Rewards don't always have to come in the form of material things or treats; a reward might be allowing them a half hour of electronics time if they complete their homework right after school, or enjoying a family movie night after a great week. Their self-esteem and worth will increase when they know what their expectations are.

Roles and expectations are so freeing because suddenly, you have full control over what happens. For example, if I choose to make my bed, I will be rewarded; if I don't, I won't be allowed to watch TV tonight. Which choice do I prefer?

When roles and expectations are fully understood and people are held accountable, they start completing tasks on their own. This strategy becomes an accepted lifestyle for children, and it won't take long for your household to run itself with minimal supervision.

Quickly, you begin to see the tangible results of your effective parenting. You are raising young people who will someday go out into the world, living their life based in the foundation you gave them. It is an amazing feeling to see your stepchildren progress while feeling loved and belonging.

With the extra time, energy, and mind space you acquire from setting your home up to regulate itself, what will you do? Perhaps you will spend extra time with your partner, pick up a hobby, or try something new. You won't even have to feel guilty for it, because your role has shifted from parenting in chaos to parenting in structure. Instead of one family emergency after another, it becomes calm waters and smooth sailing. This is not to say you won't have any more blended family drama—you will—but this time, you have the mind space and structure to deal with it.

Attribute #55: Fulfill Your Responsibilities as Part of the Team

Everybody has their own responsibilities that must be fulfilled, whether it's taking out the garbage, planning meals, or walking the dog. When the household chores are set up in a chart format and everybody knows their role, the tasks are no longer heaped onto one person (usually, that's you, the stepmom).

Why not start *including* the kids when doing household chores? You can split up the tasks, making it more reasonable. Simply giving your children small daily chores helps them learn responsibility and experience immediate results from their actions. It is more pleasant and empowering to independently maintain a clean bedroom you can have a restful sleep in, than to wait for someone else to do it.

You can also reduce your workload by promoting positive family values and by accepting help from the other household (this does not make you weak!), whether this means sharing taxing responsibilities on your "off-kid days," or collaborating to solve your child's problem over the phone. Once you can shift past your (normal) negative feelings of inadequacy or resentment from allowing the other household to help, you begin to feel a true sense that *you* are doing what's best for your child.

If you chose to maintain the mentality of "I can do it all myself, and I *will* do it all myself," you will soon burn out. Reach out to other loving, supportive people from time to time and allow them to help you. After divorce, you might feel the need to prove you can do it all yourself; however, you are hurting your children and yourself by doing it this way. Your children will benefit much more when their other parent (and the other parent's family) is involved as much as possible.

Attribute #56: Develop Feelings of Belonging

Feeling like you belong in a family means different things to different people. Knowing your roles and responsibilities, and having accountability will prove you are doing your part. When you lack purpose within your family, you might feel as though you don't belong. For example, if a child only visits Dad and Stepmom four days a month, and Stepmom does everything for the child for the entire time they are visiting (from cleaning their room to getting them a drink), they may feel like a guest in Dad's home instead of belonging in their family. So how can the child develop a sense of belonging as Dad's son or daughter, too?

When your stepchildren arrive for visitation, you shouldn't feel like you are doing everything by yourself; this will lead to anger and resentment, which are both detrimental to your relationships. Involve the children when making dinner, washing dishes, and so forth. Though they may protest at first, they will learn to appreciate helping because contributing to family tasks gives them purpose. When everyone has a role and pulls their weight, they feel belonging; they are no longer just guests.

If your family is nowhere near this vision yet, it's okay; it simply means we have to backtrack further and undo issues that may be unknowingly residing in family members. Remember, divorce has many different effects on different personalities, genders, birth orders, etc. Fortunately, we can work through this.

Another thing you can do to create a sense of belonging is to have many happy pictures on the walls, along with art projects that the kids have made over the years. When the children come and see them, they are reminded that they belong and that your household does not neglect them in their absence at the other parent's home. When we feel a sense of belonging, we are more likely to participate as a team, which is what every family needs.

Question #15: Establishing a Family Hierarchy That Helps Social Skills to Develop

Attribute #57: Understand the Detrimental Effects of Parental Alienation

If one parent decides to isolate the other parent from the child, whether due to resentment, superiority, or simply anger, they are potentially damaging the child's self-esteem and worth. Isolating them seems the easiest way to get revenge and maintain some sort of control in a broken situation, but this is not good for anyone involved in the long run.

Please don't fall into this trap. Unless there is emotional or physical abuse occurring, the parent has every right to see their child and vice-versa. In order to thrive in their new environment without both parents physically present, children *need* both parents in their lives; they need the protection, guidance, perspective, and love that is provided.

Your stepchild is half their mom and half their dad. If Mom or Dad becomes isolated, the children will begin to isolate that side of themselves by default; they may even end up hating that part of themselves. They will never feel whole if you don't let them love and be loved by their other parent.

If Mom and Dad are responsible, loving parents, they need to be in their child's life. Unless danger, abuse, or untreated mental health issues are present, both parents must set aside their pride and allow the child access to both parents. If both parents can provide a safe and loving environment, then the children must have access to both homes. If one parent does not have an environment suitable for keeping the children for extended visits, consider setting up visitation time for them to meet and spend quality time together.

Attribute #58: Maintain Respect for Both Parents of the Child

Earlier in this book, we learned about respecting people's realities: every person has their own reality, and it is important to accept, honor, and respect others for their being. If you can do that, then you are respecting your child's other parent, even if you disagree with their parenting tactics. Maintaining respect means refraining from criticism, contempt, defensiveness, and stonewalling.

Putting down the other parent in front of your child makes the child feel badly for loving that parent, guilty for seeming disloyal, and shameful for both. These damaging feelings begin percolating inside their tummies day after day, eventually leading to potential low self-esteem, low self-worth, anxiety, depression, rebellion, and many other manifestations. Criticism of either parent is also a personal criticism; we don't always consciously realize that children are internalizing this message, but they are.

By respecting each other, you can accept and honor each other's lives, and understand that each person shows up with different thoughts, experiences, and realities from your own—but this doesn't make them wrong. Normalizing and respecting each other's realities will go a long way toward promoting harmony in both families.

Attribute #59: Work with Your Partner as Heads of the Household

Part of creating and maintaining a solid foundation for your family is nurturing and supporting your relationship with your partner. Working together as a team teaches your children the same good principles that you are using in your marriage. Having established, unified leadership roles with your partner as the highest point in the hierarchy of the family is imperative to managing your blended family successfully.

Your kids will see you and their dad as their role models, which will help them learn what they need to know about how the real world works. When they enter the workforce and see authority figures at work, they will know how to respond respectively and effectively. They will learn good socialization skills, respectful manners, and how to be a team player and an honest citizen.

These gifts you give them will ultimately give them a better life. They will be able to listen to their bodies, know when something isn't right, and act while continuing to love themselves and know that they are worthy.

Attribute #60: Maintain Feelings of Safety & Security for the Children

The children are important, but they need to know that Stepmom and Dad are in charge. When children realize that no matter how much they push, their parents won't budge on certain things, this creates subconscious feelings of safety and security —essential after divorce. To feel that they can trust their parents and anticipate stable, loving actions and reactions gives them comfort and a sense of belonging.

We all have experienced when children (or even our-selves) test boundaries. For example, when they demand a new video game, how can you lovingly express your understanding but remain firm? In our home, we set goals with our children. Work with your children to determine what they need to accomplish in order to obtain what they want. Yes, this takes time, commitment, and effort, but it teaches them to work for what they want and to reward themselves afterward.

Element #4:
Creating Your Desired Reality Through Personal & Family Growth

When governance in the home is created and applied, the home begins to run itself smoothly. Now, everyone knows their roles and responsibilities, as well as the consequences for not following through. Less policing is necessary, resulting in less conflict and more positive energy.

Now that we have created more mind space and energy in each member and the unit, everyone can begin to explore themselves and participate in hobbies and interests without the stress that existed before. Your true selves begin to blossom without as much pain and stress hindering your growth and development as individuals and as a blended family.

Our youngest child is always testing our limits. Sometimes she purposely does things (knowing we won't approve) just to ensure our reactions are consistent between each other and with previous occurrences. For example, she will purposely leave her bed unmade in the morning just to see if anyone notices. She knows Dad rarely notices, but on the day that he does, she's caught!

She knows she will automatically lose one dollar from her allowance, or time on her precious iPod, but that the consequence is not a reflection of our love for her; it is simply our family plan that we are adhering to. Due to our consistent response, she realized that if she just does what's expected the first time, everyone is further ahead. Now I rarely check her bed—I know it's made!

Question #16: How Do New Rules & Governance Improve Your Family?

Attribute #61: Apply the Rules

Earlier, we discussed the creation of *your* family's plan: a developed list of mutually agreed-upon roles, responsibilities, and regulations. In our home, we held a family meeting to discuss these elements and account for everyone's input. Ultimately, my husband and I had the last say.

It was a fun exercise that brought us much closer together. We were forced to listen and *hear* each other's thoughts and feelings. The kids had fun imagining what would transpire when they 1) followed the plan and 2) when they didn't. We found that they described and proposed harsher punishments for themselves in the event boundaries were crossed than we would have.

As parents, we need to apply rules. This is about effective leadership and guidance for your kids. You must commit to following your own rules if you expect your kids to follow theirs. If you waver, they will waver. What if the kids say, "Well, we don't have to do *that* at Mom's house"? This situation will make you feel guilty and perhaps inferior to the other parent, as if your stepchild would rather not be in your home. The simple solution: say, "We aren't at Mom's house right now; we are in *our* home with *our* family plan that *we* agreed to." Again, by committing to and showing unwavering support for your family's plan, you prove to the children that their environment is predictable and secure.

Attribute #62: Teach Your Stepchildren by Allowing Natural Consequences to Occur

There are natural positive and negative consequences attached to every decision we make in life. With your stepchildren, it's okay to allow natural consequences to occur , even if it is uncomfortable for them. For example, if you take your stepdaughter to her soccer game and she forgets her water bottle in the truck, then she's simply going to have to 1) go back and get it, or 2) play without it. If you choose to return to your truck for the water, she is more likely to forget her water next time. By having to deal with the natural consequence herself, she is motivated to take responsibility for her water bottle, and thus experiences increased confidence and self-sufficiency.

Another example is your stepson forgetting his homework assignment at school. Would you normally drive back and pick it up for him? Instead, try allowing the natural consequence to occur by having him explain to his teacher why he cannot turn in his assignment. This way, he is less likely to forget his future assignments, and he feels better about himself because he spoke up and took responsibility.

In blended families, parents are already feeling guilty for having burdened their children with their divorce. It is normal to want to prevent your child from experiencing any further pain or discomfort. However, we must continue to parent our children the way we would have, had divorce not occurred. Ensure that you acknowledge the positive consequences equally, if not more so than the negative ones. If your stepchildren diligently practice for their school music recital, positive consequences will include performing well, feeling accomplishment, and being congratulated.

Help your stepchildren to recognize positive consequences, rather than only noticing the negative ones. When implementing your family rules, reinforce positive behavior with positive consequences, especially when natural positive consequences are indirect or delayed. Have a list of positive and negative consequences ready for relative actions. Let them know what to expect so they can determine their own behavior. Using natural consequences as much as possible helps your stepchildren to learn how their decisions (the cause) impact them (the effect).

Attribute #63: Create Family Culture & Tradition

Your family plan ensures that everybody recognizes their expectations and understands what is expected of them. Suddenly, everyone begins to subconsciously adapt their behavior to their environment because they want to feel belonging. This transpires into the natural, accepted culture within your household. As the Ikea television commercial says, "Everybody has their family rules." Those rules create a sense of belonging, which helps kids to increase their self-esteem, get along with others, and feel love and belonging.

As a result, everyone begins feeling more comfortable at home. There is less friction, people are having fun with each other, and you find extra time and energy. You know what is expected of you and you know whether you are fulfilling your role. Your new family culture becomes familiar, loving, and safe; perhaps for the first time, you feel as though everything just might work out.

Attribute #64: Reach Calm, Content Behavior & Communication

Now your family plan is rolling along and family members are beginning to experience measurable safety and security. You are finally fitting in with each other, and it feels comfortable; you can't wait to get home at night to see your family. Although rules may seem restrictive in the beginning, they actually give each person more personal freedom. Having a routine becomes possible; your stepchildren know that when they wake up in the morning, they are expected to make their bed and help make breakfast.

Your stepchildren now know that if they make a mistake, you will still love them unconditionally, even if they break the heel of your expensive shoes. They don't constantly worry anymore about needing to be perfect to receive love in their blended family after the loss of their first family. Now they *know* they are accepted, they are loved, and they are safe. It's very empowering to know that you are able to meet realistic expectations, and that, despite what obstacles may arise, you are always loved.

Question #17: How Will Feeling the Discomfort & Staying the Course Help?

Attribute #65: When Every Change Is Met with Resistance

Changing the rules won't be easy at first. In a blended family, difficult changes for everyone involved in and outside the home are happening all at once.

There will always be some resistance from your stepchildren (or you and your husband) when you create new expectations, especially if it is highly unfavorable, such as no longer allowing everyone to eat ice cream every single night. Perhaps your stepchildren did that in their former living arrangement and don't want that tradition to change. It is normal for people to resist change and to feel uncertainty about the unknown—in order to create and maintain the harmonious spirit in your home through these changes, it is vital that the plan is followed from its first implementation.

Blended families have a unique experience with change, because more unfavorable change comes with extra feelings of guilt; parents don't want their children suffering any further discomfort after the divorce. Though normal, it can be incredibly painful for parents to see their children in even more distress post-divorce, even if it is something they *know* they should be enforcing, like not allowing ice cream every day.

Attribute #66: Deal with Fear, Guilt, & Potential Instability

Stand by what you say, and don't waiver. Stick with your husband and support each other through change. Resistance will occur in the beginning. If you need a sounding board, talk to someone who has already been there or who can empathize with you. You need to know that what you're experiencing is normal; once you normalize your feelings, you can deal with them and move on. This will allow you to make wise, constructive decisions for your blended family.

It's easy to become consumed by and lost in your emotions. You must realize that when you waver because *you* feel terrible that your child is resisting, you are selfishly stunting their development. Part of your job as a parent is to allow your child to safely experience and navigate negative emotions while maintaining healthy boundaries.

For example, if you've chosen to hold dessert night in your home on Fridays to promote healthier eating, then it only happens Fridays (with the exception of special events). If your child has a temper tantrum on Monday night because she desperately wants something sweet, explore this with her. This does not mean give her a dessert because you can't stand to see her unhappy post-divorce.

Explore her feelings with her: Why is she craving? Is she dehydrated? Is she feeling lonely? Did something happen at school? Take the time and be with her to reassure her that you're there, you care, and you will solve the problem together.

Shoving dessert in her mouth to make her stop crying is only helping yourself—so you don't have to feel the discomfort and guilt. Allowing your children to run wild without any rules doesn't help them, and justifying your behavior of giving in will only hold you all back.

Wavering on your family plan does not help your child. Our ultimate goal as parents is to nurture and prepare your children for the world. By not abiding by your own rules that you have set together, you're teaching them that they don't have to follow rules in life—and we know that's simply not the case. Parenting is challenging, but I know you're up for it!

Attribute #67: Maintain Stability in Your Marriage through Change

You and your husband must be on the same page. As soon as your stepchildren spot weakness in your chain, they will attempt to break the chain. They do this to test their new environment—to see if this family will break up like the last one. You cannot allow them to break the foundation that you and your husband have engineered. If they succeed, the stability and security you have strived to produce is threatened in their minds.

Having an effective family and co-parenting plan will deliver significant benefits to your children, your marriage, and your relationship with the other family. If the other family opts out of having a co-parenting plan, it's okay; you can still manage your home with this strategy and experience positive results. Especially in cases where a co-parenting plan is not in place, a family plan for your own home is imperative.

Attribute #68: Learn to Manage Your Feelings

Time will allow blended family changes to settle and become normal in your home. Each member of the family is learning to adapt at their own pace, but still requires love and nurturing. Positive changes that originate from having an effective family plan with appropriate rules and responsibilities help to remove feelings of anxiety and uncertainty, leaving room for feelings of safety, belonging, and love to take their place.

Once your stepchildren realize your seriousness of standing by the rules, and they know that they cannot get you or their dad to waver, they will start to accept the rules as normal. They *know* what is expected of them, which will guide them through change, rather than feeling upset because their perceived freedom is being taken away. Soon, they will learn that it isn't about *them*; it's about the family as a team. Your stepchildren will want to contribute because they feel loved and want to belong.

Home will start to become a desirable safe haven for everyone. The children will start to discover a true sense of belonging again after great loss, and as a stepmom, you will begin to feel less like an outsider. After all, you had a significant hand in creating this haven. This haven is especially unique if your stepchildren's parents divorced early on or if there was conflict in the home. Peace and calm may be new to them, but it is usually a welcome change met with happiness and contentment.

Question #18: How Can You Encourage the Beauty of Individuals to Emerge?

Attribute #69: Understand Where You Fit In

As your feelings of peace, contentment, and love in your day-to-day life increase, you truly begin to feel like you belong. Concurrently, each member will be feeling that same sense of belonging. When a person experiences belonging, they feel as though no matter what, they are supported, loved unconditionally, and can achieve anything. It will help each member learn who they are individually, who you are as their stepmom, and who your family is as a unit.

It's important that you feel as though you belong in your blended family as a stepmom to prevent anger and resentment. You can shift through these residual emotions caused loneliness and a feeling that you don't belong. Afterward, you can emerge as a beautiful, strong stepmom. Gaining and maintaining respect for one another can create harmony, which can later turn into true love. You will find the wonderful side of being a part of a dynamic blended family, and uncover fulfillment and love that you never knew you had.

As you proceed on this challenging journey of inner transformation, you will experience different sides of yourself that you did not know existed. You will face deep-rooted wounds from your past that have led you to this point; together, we can heal these wounds. The overall process of uniting your new blended family with a family plan—a *clear* set of roles, realistic expectations, and responsibilities—and enforcing natural consequences will make you and your husband better people. Your plan provides you all the tools needed to continue to grow and progress throughout life.

Attribute #70: Provide Positive Feedback & Reinforcement

Earlier, we discussed positive reinforcement, which is simple yet effective, and one of the best tools that you can use as a stepparent. Giving positive reinforcement means acknowledging and reinforcing positive things that are occurring in day-to-day life. Essentially, you are noticing, recognizing, and rewarding the good that you see all over the home. When you begin focusing on the positives, your stepchildren will follow suit, even if it's as simple as celebrating the pass they made during their soccer game. Noticing + Acknowledging + Rewarding = Good feelings all around!

Children benefit from positive reinforcement because it continuously reassures them that they are walking a great path and making wise choices. By embracing positivity, you are shifting the culture of your family to a better and higher perspective. Don't make this strategy solely about your stepchildren's achievements; also celebrate and encourage other positive behavior from all family members, including being kind to someone who has been bullied at school, helping with yard work, sharing a gift with a sibling, and showing initiative at home and in the community.

Any of that can be rewarded, even if the reward is a simple, "Jason, I noticed you were helping your siblings with their chores today. I'm proud of you for showing that you care," or, "Lacey, I heard that you've been tutoring the other kids in science class. I really admire you for doing that."

Attribute #71: See How People Thrive by Meeting & Exceeding Expectations

As you integrate these processes into your daily life, you begin experiencing new elements of your own personality that you didn't realize were there—even as an adult. I'm a completely different adult now than I was before I became a stepmother. Now, I'm a better person: kinder, more compassionate, and more tolerant. I also realize that little details really don't matter so much. My blended family truly makes me want to be better, and I appreciate their support.

It's helpful to set personal goals for yourself to help you realize and meet *realistic* expectations of yourself inside and outside of your family. Goal-setting encourages us and our children to imagine what we want out of life and to go for it. Goals keep us moving in a positive direction to meet our ultimate wants and needs. They keep us accountable and feeling good about ourselves after small and larger accomplishments. If you know what each of your family members' goals are, you can help each other to achieve them, thereby giving you similar purposes and feeling more connected.

Attribute #72: Provide Regular, Structured Space for People to Become Themselves & Flourish

Today, many parents overburden their children with extracurricular activities, electronics, and mind-numbing activities (such as video games). These activities are great in moderation but can be abused. In addition to overstimulation, parents are concurrently pushing their children to do well in school and meet their expectations at home (and rightly so).

However, there is such a thing as *too much* structure; it's necessary that you encourage your children during "free time" each day so they can figure out who *they* are, what *they* like to do, and what they *want* to do. Kids are rushed from one activity to the next, scrambling to do their homework and eat something before bedtime, and then simply hitting repeat the next day. Wouldn't it be nice to see them explore by themselves instead of us dictating their schedule?

While many parents are accustomed to planning every minute of their child's day "to keep them busy," it is beneficial to take a step back and allow your children to figure out what they want to do. It's important that kids have some of their own time to explore and discover who they are as people. If your child has a difficult time occupying themselves with something they enjoy, they likely don't know what they enjoy yet. It can be uncomfortable to see your child complain of boredom. As parents, we can offer suggestions, support, and resources to help them figure it out, but ultimately, they need to explore by themselves to determine what they like.

Question #19: Why Should You Recognize the Contributions of Each Individual in the Family?

Attribute #73: Create a Safe, Structured Environment

Safety and structure allows parents to be parents and kids to be kids. When we began inviting other kids over to play, the parents would ask what I would *do* with the kids during their visit. "What activities do you have planned?" or "What are we going to do at this play date?" Or the parents would say, "Well, what activities do you have planned for today?" And I'd stun them with my simple answer of "Nothing."

"What do you mean, 'nothing'? What are they going to do all day? What are you going to do to keep them occupied?" the parents would ask.

"I'm not going to do anything. I'm going to put them outside, supervise them from inside, and I'm going to watch them play."

When you have rules and expectations in place, kids understand what behavior is acceptable; that lets them focus on being kids. They are free to play because they have boundaries. When they test or go beyond their boundaries, they either learn from it on their own, experience a natural negative consequence, or the parents step in to enforce a planned consequence.

They learn best by experimenting in a safe and secure environment; you provide that by giving them boundaries and expectations. Children learn to make their own decisions through cause and effect, and they have room to be their own person.

When you don't have to spend every second hovering over your children, maybe you could enjoy a conversation or glass of wine with your husband, and that's okay. You're providing room for your children to gain autonomy, improve their social skills, get to know themselves, and increase their confidence.

Attribute #74: Share Skills, Natural Talents, & Interests

While you're allowing these changes to unfold naturally, you have newfound time and energy to notice the raw talents each of you possess. Ask yourself what skills and talents each of you bring to the family unit. How is each family member different? How do they contribute to the family? How will they excel individually?

When you begin to realize the talents and skills of each family member, you can accentuate each person's individual attributes by relating their family tasks to what they are good at. For example, my eldest stepdaughter enjoys configuring electronics, so this is her job in our home.

This natural skill of hers may have gone unnoticed (or may never have surfaced) if we remained stuck in blended family drama and neglected to put a strong family structure and plan in place. When you don't have family structure, *anything goes*. Kids have no idea what's expected of them: what they're supposed to do, where they're supposed to be, or who they are. This leads to uncertainty at home, low confidence in themselves, and overall anxiety.

When they have the opportunity, time, and space to figure out their natural skills, they may realize, "Okay, I don't like English class, but I really like reading. So I'm going to read 100 books this year and I will report whether they were good or not." (This was Kara's goal when she was 8, and she reached it!) It is so inspiring to see your stepchildren discover their talents and abilities.

Attribute #75: Let Everyone Start Being Themselves

Now that your home is running itself, everyone can start to feel like home is the safest place in the world. Home is where you can be yourself and know your family will have your back no matter what.

Schoolyard bullying is a hot topic right now. Imagine your stepchild has recently experienced their parents divorcing, is feeling alone and hurt, and on top of that, is getting bullied at school. . . Where in their world are they finding solace? Regardless of whether they *are* being bullied at school or not, it is your job as parents to provide a safe, loving home without unnecessary additional stress.

Do you want to be able to provide a safe haven where you and your children can rest and become strong for the challenges ahead? Some kids (especially in blended families) deal with bullies at school, arrive home to experience more conflict, and then experience more conflict and stress the following school day.

For these kids, there is no break. This unrelenting stressful environment is detrimental to the child's growth and development, and is entirely avoidable. It takes strong parents to step up after divorce, set their needs aside, and do what is best for their families.

When you can instill a sense of safety and security in your home, and the stress and drama experienced during divorce begins to disintegrate, you begin to see a new, wonderful side of your children. They are no longer scared, wounded, and uncertain of the future; now, they trust you and their family.

Attribute #76: Relax—the House Is Managing Itself

With the rules and expectations in place, chaos no longer rules your home, and your kids have a safe refuge to return to. If your stepchildren are experiencing trouble in their lives outside of the home (even as they morph into teens), they are more likely to report it and seek guidance from an adult who will intervene. They will feel safe enough to share their deepest fears and problems with you.

Increased love and security at home will nudge them forward to get help with any problems they may have—whether it's a bully at school, difficulty in class, or problems with friends, sex, drugs, or anything else. When kids feel safe to open up, they are more likely to go to their parents or stepparents and admit they need help. Do you think a child or young adult will seek guidance from you if your home is in blended emotional chaos?

When you have established a strong structure and positive family culture, the house practically manages itself. Chores are completed because everyone knows what is expected of them and people are feeling good for contributing. As the stepmom, you benefit a lot because many small, disregarded tasks fell in your lap, but now, you have help! The chores are getting done without you having to say, "Put your laundry away," because one of the rules is that each person puts away their own laundry to get their allowance.

Question #20: How Can You Gain Family Support to Achieve Your Personal Goals?

Attribute #77: Decrease Household & Co-Parenting Stress by Showing Support

Decreased levels of stress enable life's everyday challenges to become easier for everyone to cope, especially you, the stepmom. Along with reduced stress overall, you end up with extra time and energy that you can gear toward things you actually *want* to do, rather than constantly doing things for others. You get to take a break and be you.

Having co-parenting measures in place (if possible) results in a similar transformation; you and your husband become more relaxed, and the other family also becomes more relaxed. You can all learn to have peace, knowing you're working together to raise wonderful children.

Attribute #78: Use Your Freed-Up Energy on Personal Growth

With all of that extra energy, you can now do new, fun and interesting things more often. You can volunteer, join a club, organize an event, take your husband on a date. . . you can do many things! Not only do you get the energy to do more things, but you also get a boost in physical health and overall well-being from feeling good. Perhaps you want to lose weight, learn a new language, make some new friends, or attend yoga classes; the sky is the limit. You owe this to yourself and your blended family; you need to be happy and healthy to be "*on*" for them.

Think about how you have transformed your thinking just by reading this alternate way of managing your blended family. Isn't it amazing? There are so many possibilities for you to become who *you* were meant to be, to serve the purpose *you* were born to serve. Although you possibly came to me from constant blended family conflict, drama, and turmoil—perhaps even *hating* your steplife and wishing your husband's ex-wife didn't exist—now your thoughts and intentions have shifted to a more positive outlook with limitless possibilities.

It's amazing what will transpire through this process and how much your life will improve. With your energy levels higher and your outlook more positive, there is less room for rumination or regret. We've learned to 1) cope with and manage our personal wounds acquired prior to our blended families, 2) recognize our triggers and understand their deeper meaning for us, 3) apply a family plan to our blended family, and 4) lift each other up instead of tearing each other down.

Attribute #79: Make Goals as a Family

Part of enjoying family life is by starting fun, unforgettable family traditions, which always excites everyone and increases that good feeling of cohesiveness to your family. Your new traditions could be as simple as devoting one day during Christmas holidays to watching movies in your new Christmas pajamas while enjoying delicious fondue. Or your traditions could be more elaborate, like traveling to Algonquin Park every summer for camping, bonfires, and hikes.

This is where you can really start to make fun goals as individuals and as a family, and you can support each other in reaching goals.

It becomes so nice when everyone is participating and actually wants to do things together. You can start by exploring each other's dreams and go from there. For example, when I look to the future, I see our family, traditions, and home as the place my stepdaughters want to bring their friends, new boyfriends, and, someday, their own families to share how wonderful their childhood was.

Attribute #80: Have Mutual Respect & Love People for Who They Are

Creating and achieving goals together allows you to blossom as an individual to a much higher level; you begin from a different place of respect and support. Throughout this process of creating and achieving goals together, acknowledging each other's raw talents, and helping each other reach goals, a newfound love and respect will emerge.

When they're your biological kids, there is an implied feeling of unconditional love that is innate because you share blood. In your blended family, however, natural love will not exist without commitment and effort.

You may feel love for your stepchildren in this moment, or you may not. Either way, that's okay! Love can come later when you take the time to learn who the child is, separate from their wounds and behavior from the divorce.

This kind of love is so special because it comes from a genuine, selfless place that you shaped. Having mutual respect and love encourages belonging. Each person in the family gets the opportunity to shine as an individual and share their talents and skills with the family team.

Element #5:

Cultivating Love & Appreciation For Yourself & Your Blended Family

By relying on the family management system that you have in place, you can become more adaptable and tolerant of the uncertainty in life. The time saved by using your system can be used to grow and develop as individuals and as a family. New traditions can be formed, giving members a sense of love and belonging. Unconditional love and respect follows.

On the first Christmas we spent together as a family, I asked our kids what one special activity they wanted to do throughout the holidays. They insisted that we spend one day in our pajamas playing board games, watching movies, and having fondue for dinner. It was a fun day even though I hadn't thought of it as being traditional.

The following year, our kids began planning our annual family "PJ and fondue party" without prompting. It had been their most memorable activity last Christmas. Now, we enjoy this tradition every year. It makes us feel like we belong together in our home, increasing our unconditional love for each other.

Question #21: How Can You Adapt to Unexpected Events?

Attribute #81: Rely on the System to Manage the Unforeseen Events

Every day, we are faced with challenges; this is just life. When you have a family structure in place, it is much easier to handle unforeseen events. Chaos makes everyday challenges much more unbearable; when you are trying to manage daily events on top of chaos, you can never seem to accomplish anything no matter what you do.

By having this structure in place, it's easier to succeed, even when you experience unforeseen events, and you will see unexpected events begin to manage themselves.

Eventually, you will know that you *can* count on your family system to get you and your family through anything; you can rely on the structure, rules, and guidelines in place, as well as each person involved. When you develop that level of trust, it really changes the shape and magnitude of everyday problems.

Attribute #82: Perceive "Problems" as Opportunities for Personal & Familial Growth

When they lack structure, kids take on their parents' adult issues. While newly divorced parents become caught up in a toxic cyclone of blended family drama, they don't realize that everything they say and do is affecting their children. Children take on adult issues by default when they don't have room at home to be kids; they naturally want to please their parents and decrease their stress. When parents are extra stressed and aren't managing their stress in healthy ways, kids automatically wear that stress, too.

As the kids age and you mature, different blended family issues will arise. It is fascinating to see how your kids learn to deal with their own issues, leaving less up to you as they become more independent. This shift gives you more time to deal with the present adult issues, and your kids have more energy to deal with their own age-related issues.

Implementing structure in your home gives you the space to deal with your adult issues, and the children the space to deal with age-appropriate issues. Kids get to be kids, and the adults can resolve their issues in a healthy way rather than imposing their problems on others.

When your stepchildren are focusing on their own age-related problems rather than their parents' worries, they can better enjoy being a kid. Without being dragged down by anxiety about adult issues, they have more friends, get better grades in school, and feel happier, confident, and more alive. This, of course, benefits everybody, and it's all because there is adequate structure in place.

Attribute #83: Develop Unconditional Respect

This attribute of a healthy blended family was hinted at in the previous chapter. If you want your family to work effectively, mutual respect for one another *must* be developed. In blended families, you may never achieve real feelings of unconditional love for your stepchildren— and that's okay. In many cases, this is perfectly normal. If you absolutely love your stepchildren even though your stepchildren do not love you back to the same degree, you can still have a very healthy respect for each other.

Once you achieve mutual respect, you have improved the fluid movement of activity within the home. Respect flows in all directions. Your stepchildren begin to respect your space because you have enforced boundaries that they honor; when your stepchildren see that you won't waver under their pressure, they feel trust and security (even when they aren't getting *their way*). Once you see your stepchildren trying really hard to be respectful, you end up loving and respecting each child just because they are trying to fit in and please you. It's a wonderful feeling.

Attribute #84: Enjoy the Feeling of Belonging No Matter What

Even if we don't achieve feelings of true love with our stepchildren that exist in biological families, it is still possible to find belonging and mutual respect. This respect and belonging stems from knowing that no matter what happens, you will still be together.

This is really important for a child after divorce; they have lost that sense of security as a child. Their root beliefs about family have been tested, and they question whether new people in their lives will remain there; after all, they have already lost fulltime access to both Mom and Dad. Although their biological parents might be there emotionally, they cannot always be there physically after divorce. Everyone needs to feel they belong somewhere, no matter what.

Question #22: Is Your Relationship with Your Partner the Foundation of Your Family?

The foundation between you and your partner is necessary for this structure to work. At this stage, you're actually reaping the benefits, restoring your good, strong relationship that you and the children respect.

Attribute #85: Keep Your Marriage Strong with Regular Maintenance

At this point, you and your partner actually have the time and the energy to do relationship maintenance. When you are in blended family turmoil, spending time together and keeping the home fires burning are not your highest priorities, though they should be. Following this system will give you and your partner the time, energy, and respect necessary for the whole family to want to spend quality time together.

Scheduling a quality time date night weekly where you can reconnect with your partner will make a significant difference in your marriage and respect for each other. Every day, you should spend at least 20 minutes checking in with each other to ensure that you are still working together from the same page.

We started these activities in the beginning and realized how effective they were after we stopped doing them for a month. That's all it took for family life to become chaotic! When you don't participate in weekly meetings, the whole system can really fall apart. The kids totally feel it, and they know that you are not as strongly connected. Once you realize how much these check-ins help with the flow of day-to-day operation, you won't ever want to neglect weekly meetings with your partner again.

When you begin to experience your triggers or feel anger or resentment arising, it's time to stop and reassess the situation. How are you feeling? Have you shared this with your partner? Have you been taking care of yourself, or only others? Your relationship with yourself needs just as much TLC as your relationship with your hubby.

Attribute #86: Cultivate Unconditional Love for Each Other as Partners

Second marriages are difficult to begin with; this is normal. You now have a wonderful opportunity to become true partners in life, but also best friends, confidants, and family who deeply respect and love each other. You have common familial goals of having and maintaining a good relationship, healthy children, and a beautiful family that belongs together. Belonging develops from reaching a stage of interconnectedness, an infinitely deeper level or connection than just dating.

Despite any obstacles that arise, you are committed to the challenge of keeping your love alive. Once you arrive on this level, you will never go back. You will never let your relationship slip down the priority list again, because you are so happy in your current place.

At that point, nothing can shake you. Your love for yourself and one another is so great and so necessary that it becomes unconditional. Even if you get into a big argument, you know that you have enough love and respect for each other to overcome it; time will heal our wounds if we actively participate in the healing process. You now feel comfortable enough to respectfully discuss your feelings and issues without feeling threatened. From there, you can build a new level of strength and security in your relationship that will last a lifetime.

Attribute #87: Increase Feelings of Safety & Security in Your Children

Now, you are uncovering increased feelings of safety and security experienced by the children, which they feel as a result of you and Dad creating a safe home for them. The source of the glue holding the family together does not come from the rules anymore, but from the feeling of security and belonging in your family. You become unconsciously loyal to each other, enough that you want to put their needs and goals ahead of your own.

When everybody is building each other up like this, you can accomplish really amazing things. This is a milestone you will reach by build loyalty in your blended family. It is possible for your family, and it's totally wonderful. Once you have *built it*—because you didn't just inherit it—you have done it. That gives you a gratifying sense of achievement.

Attribute #88: Root Your Family in Unconditional Love

The difference between natural families versus stepfamilies is that natural families automatically have unconditional love for their children before they even enter the world. In blended families, unconditional love takes time, commitment, patience, perseverance, and even trial and error.

Once you have achieved respect in a blended family, you are halfway there! Imagine reaching a state of unconditional love with your stepchildren even though they are not your natural children. It's different than a biological mother-child relationship; even if Mom isn't in the picture, it's still different. It's truly a special feeling when you can learn to love people in your blended family that don't share your DNA.

When unconditional love becomes the core of your family, uncertainty that existed during times away from your stepchildren (such as when they visit their other parent) begin to fade; they always return from their visit to the safe environment that you provide where everyone is valued. Your stepchildren return to unconditional love rather than scrambling to establish your authority after visiting their other parent. Everything runs much more smoothly when love is at the center of your family.

When my stepdaughters return from Mom's, they know that nothing has changed; it is still the same "boring old Kait and Dad," which is great. This makes it so much easier and more fun for everyone. They may call us "boring old Kait and Dad," but it's a blessing because it means they feel stable and secure, and they can joke about it without retribution. We know that they love being home and having a predictable environment that gives them security resulting from knowing exactly what to expect when they return.

Question #23: How Does Strong Leadership Steer the Direction of Your Family?

Attribute #89: Express Feelings without Judgment or Limitation

After implementing your family plan and spending the time to develop patience and compassion, you arrive at a place where anyone in the family can respectfully say how they feel. Each person can say exactly what is on their mind without feeling judged.

We can now deal with issues as they come up on a daily basis, the same way that a biological family does, rather than dealing with blended family stress and chaos on top of pressing issues. When strong leadership skills are instilled in children, the family runs itself, and you can have non-judgmental discussions about the sensitive issues because you know that you belong.

Family members now feel as if they can voice their opinion and it will be heard; they no longer feel the need to suppress their inner voice. Even if the conversation is one you don't want to be a part of, you can empathize and understand that your family member needs to release this information. Because you have reached unconditional love and respect for your family, it is much easier to listen to each other's thoughts, feelings, strengths, weaknesses, and limitations with an open mind and heart. It benefits everyone to be in an environment where you can be you.

Remember, every day in a blended family is different. A 6-year-old child will feel one way about the divorce and new marriage, but when they become 10, they may feel completely different. Roll with this. They may go back and forth from feeling to feeling, they may move forward or backward at times; anticipate this and don't take it personally. Expect that this will happen, because your step-children are surrounded by triggers every day, just as you are. Once you learn how to shift your own feelings from triggers, you can teach them to do the same.

Know that it is okay to love your stepchild, regardless of how they feel about you (and vice versa). People argue from time to time. For example, your stepchild may become upset and confused by different rules in different homes. This is warranted; help them work through it. You need to take the time to work through these issues just as you would in a natural family. Speaking and listening without judgment is so important for moving forward. By basing your actions and reactions in love and respect, you can achieve this.

Attribute #90: Provide Space for Kids to Be Kids

Adult issues are unintentionally imposed on children because they are always around, always listening, and always hoping to imitate us. They see us when we are stressed and when we argue. Whether it's between households or within the home, that conflict stresses them. Kids (even teens) have fewer developed coping mechanisms to deal with stress, thus producing more internal and external challenges.

When you have a good family structure in place, along with mutual respect and compassion, it is much easier for everyone to overcome challenges. It creates more energy, better balance, and improved mental space—not just for the kids, but also for the adults. Adult issues are for the adults; let the kids be kids!

Attribute #91: Help Children Relate to Their Own Age Group & Regain Their Childhood after Divorce

Children see how other kids behave, they watch movies depicting kid-parent relationships, and they can sense when other kids are struggling. Kids talk to and about each other, they know each other's backgrounds.

Eventually, children of divorce (especially the oldest children) may realize that they are emotionally more mature than the other kids at school. They may lack similarities and common interests and thus begin to withdraw.

When adults attach their issues to their child, the issues hang off the child like a ball and chain all day long. Having relationships with children who are the stepchild's same age therefore proves to be challenging.

Especially as a single parent, be conscientious of this. Refrain from using your child as an emotional crutch.

While it is understandable how difficult life can be when you are single and working full time on top of your home duties, you cannot let this impact the way you parent. Your issues are yours; if you need help, get adult help. This will allow your child to be a kid and thrive at an age-appropriate rate.

Regardless of divorce, children can recuperate and live normal lives without additional, unnecessary stress. They can continue to relate to children their own age without being "10 going on 30" from the emotional stress that they have been forced to manage. Allow them that space.

Attribute #92: See That Anything Becomes Possible for Your Future

As a child, you don't have a grasp of the future, nor do you really care. This is the beauty of childhood; you can fly by the seat of your pants carelessly while exploring yourself. If your stepchildren come home to chronic stress and conflict, it can take over their brain to the point where they don't do well in school, they cannot relate to kids their own age, and they may be ostracized by other kids because they are different.

It is difficult for a child to understand why they are not accepted by their peers. In fact, they might never understand until they are older, have found balance in their lives, and are no longer chronically stressed. (As an adult, once you realize this, you can look back at your childhood and acknowledge, "Oh, that's why I was this way," or "So *that's* why this happened.")

It is up to you and your husband to create a safe, loving environment for your kids. If they were brought up in a stressful environment, then they will still be overwhelmed and need extra nurturing.

Stress can affect young brains similarly to the way that alcohol and drug abuse affects adult brains. In addition, if your child is dealing with constant stress, they will have difficulties making friends, doing well in school, and feeling well and healthy; for example, they may experience recurrent tummy aches or illness from dealing with too much stress.

(It is important to note that a child will not necessarily know the difference between being brought up in a stressful environment if that is all they know. The physical changes in their brain development are, however, real, and will affect how capable they are of managing stress and anxiety as they grow older.)

Ideally, you and your partner will help your child to live a stress-free (within reason) life, and maintain a healthy mind and lifestyle where they can just be a kid. Let their biggest concerns in life be not getting grounded for a year after breaking your favorite lamp because they threw a ball in the house, or forgetting to get all of their homework done in time for school. As we discussed earlier, once you have the right rules, expectations, and natural consequences in place, you have developed a good structure allowing your child to be a kid.

Question #24: What Happens Next to Bring Your Blended Family a Good Life?

With your family plan in place, stress is being alleviated throughout your life in and out of the home.

Attribute #93: Look Ahead

Kids, especially those under 10, tend to remember what they are prompted to remember. When you have fun family traditions and memories, they will reminisce: "Yes, I remember that. It was fun. I want to do that again."

When they share their family traditions and memories with friends, they can relate to other kids in natural families. Often, when chaos exists, traditions are nil and memories are better left forgotten.

Before divorce, they may not have had family traditions recently because their family was preoccupied with stress. Now, however, they can experience this with you!

Even the simplest of things can bring the greatest joy to people. When you have a bad day, remind yourself of your positive family traditions and memories.

Everybody needs tradition. Family traditions give you feelings of belonging and love at home and in the community.

Attribute #94: Adapt as Needed

Now, nothing is set in stone; you can roll with whatever happens each day. If you make a rule one day, you can change it later to accommodate new circumstances. If unexpected events happen, you can keep faith in your family system and your loved ones to overcome any obstacles.

Even though today may seem unbearable, you can make tomorrow better; this, too, shall pass.

Maintaining a positive attitude helps you adapt to unexpected events. For example, what if your stepchild decided to skip school? If you don't have a blended family system plan in place and it's still a toxic environment, 1) you may not even recognize that your stepchild missed class because you are preoccupied with your own issues, and/or 2) you might overreact by projecting your stress on them without accounting for the bigger picture. But if you have a structure in place, you can actually sit down and calmly discuss the situation. You can prevent this from happening again by probing them for reasons, giving them guidance and the tools they need, and remaining rational.

Attribute #95: Know It Will All Work Out

Have faith that you can and will overcome this time in your life. Know that it will get better with effort. You can reach this mindset when you allow yourself to trust and love you, the system, and your family.

Now, it is not even the roles, rules, and responsibilities that are running the show anymore. The rules have just become the norm, the "family culture." They are not really even rules anymore because now, that is just the way things are done at home.

Attribute #96: Now, You Are Always Happy to Come Home at Night!

Home is a place where you now know there is support, things get worked out, and you can safely express your voice. There is such a healthier way for everyone to deal with life's challenges rather than avoiding coming home at night.

Many men (especially) that are unhappy at home tend to work later than they need to, drink more, and avoid conflict at all costs. At this stage, they simply feel that no matter what they do, someone isn't happy; they are at a loss.

When a man feels inadequate to fix a problem at home, he may avoid it altogether. These are signs that there is no strong foundation at home. Fortunately, men can definitely come back from this phase; it's a difficult way of living for everybody and it cannot continue in the long run.

On the other hand, a woman will always come home right after work. When conflict arises, she feels that home is where she needs to be to work things out.

As a woman, you know that if you cannot communicate appropriately with your man, he will get discouraged. Try to avoid name-calling, contempt, revenge, and other unhelpful, disrespectful tactics. As a father of divorce, your husband is already feeling a sense of failure; an unhappy new wife might be unbearable for him.

When conflict is appropriately managed, a man will be excited to come home after work. It is important that we *want* to be at home at night. Home is that special, safe place where magical things can happen. That is where you are loved, respected, and supported no matter what.

Before, you may have dreaded coming home because of your stress level and the conflict you felt with your blended family. Now, however, no matter what life throws at you, you are always happy to come home regardless. You know you can deal with it together.

Question #25: Where Can You Foster Contentment, Belonging, & Self-Worth within Your Family?

Attribute #97: See Each Other's Imperfections as Perfection

What was imperfect to you about others becomes perfect in your eyes. No matter how imperfect your blended family may seem to somebody on the outside, it's perfect to and for you; that's what matters. Blended families continue to be stigmatized throughout society, regardless of their skyrocketing numbers, but when you feel that what you have is perfect, you've found where you belong.

It's your perfect family life that you have always wanted. This is a life that you have built through intention rather than by default, and that is why it becomes so rewarding and special.

Attribute #98: Embrace Your New Reality of Love & Respect

Many of us accept our reality as it drops into our laps because it's what we were "given." In your blended family, though, your new reality of love and respect is one that you *chose* to action. At this point, how could you not love and respect each person within your family?

Even when one of your stepchildren is acting out, your learned compassion *knows* there is a deeper meaning for their reaction. You now have the tools to deal with it in a healthy way. This new reality is simply so much better! (I would never go back from this new reality, and I continue to climb into higher power daily.) Sometimes you fall, but the next day, you pick yourself up, dust yourself off, and try again.

Now, we're beyond the belief that natural families are more beneficial, because we are living it! Our blended family is just as loving and productive as a natural family. Even if you are in a natural family, you can still have the same degree of stress and turmoil.

You will only achieve this new, better reality if you build it for yourself; you cannot choose the default reality of a blended family, which is often chaos and emotional disconnect. When you can get your family to this level of love and respect, your family is operating in the 99th percentile of *families* (not stepfamilies—families). It doesn't get much better than this.

Attribute #99: Trust That People at Home Will Help You If You Fall

Everybody will fall once in a while. I still remember the day that I lost my 14-year-old Pekingese in 2013. I cried for three days straight because he had been my baby since he was six weeks old.

Although I was trying to stay strong for the girls, I was absolutely heartbroken. The way they sat beside, consoling me, and understanding that this was a healthy way for me to react with the loss of my baby, was incredible. They knew I needed to cry and mourn my dog's death.

The compassion they showed me at 7 and 9 years old was so touching. I felt closer to them than I ever had before. The way that they stood by me and cared made me feel as if I really belonged here in this family with them, even though I'm not their biological mom.

Attribute #100: Be Happy with Yourself While Each Family Member Develops Their Own Self-Love

Eventually, you end up realizing that you are loved and cared for by others because people respect the love and respect that you show yourself. When you make time to love and respect yourself, your family will love and respect you more, which, in turn, causes you to love them even more! Ultimately, you've created a dependable cycle of love and respect for all of you.

Taking care of yourself is first and foremost; then, everyone else will follow suit. If you don't take care of yourself, you cannot adequately care for others, and further, you cannot expect others to care for you. Likewise, if you don't love yourself, how can you expect to genuinely love others? It all begins with you.

Learning and implementing these real-life skills to grow and develop into your authentic self will make a world of difference in your life. The gift you receive by taking care of yourself first in your blended family is a loving marriage, the ability to build and maintain your family structure, and children whose lives you are helping to shape.

You can create this reality of love and acceptance in your own heart, which your blended family will mirror. It truly is possible to build a family with a strong foundation of unconditional love and respect, where each person is valued for their infinite worth.

www.ingramcontent.com/pod-product-compliance
Lightning Source LLC
Chambersburg PA
CBHW072202090426
42740CB00012B/2355